The Seven Sweet Blessings of Christ

Also available from
Sophia Institute Press
by Gerald Vann:

The Devil:
And How to Resist Him

Gerald Vann

The Seven Sweet Blessings of Christ

And How to Make Them Yours

SOPHIA INSTITUTE PRESS®

Manchester, New Hampshire

The Seven Sweet Blessings of Christ: And How to Make Them Yours was originally published by HarperCollins Publishers Ltd. under the title *The Divine Pity* by Gerald Vann. This 1997 edition, which includes slight revisions, is published with the permission of HarperCollins. The Author asserts the moral right to be identified as the Author of this work.

Jacket design by Joan Barger

The cover painting is a detail from *The Last Supper* by Domenico Ghirlandaio, from the monastery of San Marco, Florence, Italy.

Sophia Institute Press®
Box 5284, Manchester, NH 03108
1-800-888-9344

Nihil Obstat: Fr. Conrad Pepler, O.P., S.T.L., Fr. Columba Ryan, O.P., S.T.L.
Imprimi Potest: Fr. Benedict O'Driscoll, O.P., *Prior Provincialis Angliae*
London, September 28, 1944
Nihil Obstat: George Phillips, S.TH.L., *Censor Deputatus*
Imprimatur: E. Morrogh Bernard, *Vicarius Generalis*
Westmonasterii, July 23, 1945

Library of Congress Cataloging-in-Publication Data

Vann, Gerald, 1906-1963.
[Divine pity]
The seven sweet blessings of Christ : and how to make them yours / Gerald Vann.
p. cm.
Originally published: The divine pity. [S.l.] : HarperCollins, c1945.
Includes bibliographical references.
ISBN 0-918477-55-7 (pbk. : alk. paper)
1. Beatitudes — Devotional literature. 2. Sacraments — Catholic Church. 3. Catholic Church — Doctrines. I. Title.
BT382.V3 1997
241.5'3 — dc21 97-16979 CIP

97 98 99 00 01 02 10 9 8 7 6 5 4 3 2 1

CONTENTS

The Seven Sweet Blessings of Christ

The Beatitudes

Blessed are the poor in spirit,
for theirs is the kingdom of Heaven.

Blessed are the meek,
for they shall possess the land.

Blessed are they who mourn,
for they shall be comforted.

Blessed are they who hunger
and thirst for justice,
for they shall have their fill.

Blessed are the merciful,
for they shall obtain mercy.

Blessed are the clean of heart,
for they shall see God.

Blessed are the peacemakers,
for they shall be called the children of God.

Matt. 5:3-9

Chapter One

The Call to Love and Serve

One of the most tantalizing figures in the whole of the Gospel story is surely Lazarus, the man who for four days lay dead, and was then brought back to the world by the word of our Lord.[1] He was a man who knew by experience, who had *seen*, the answer to the questions which perpetually engage the human mind: the nature of the world that awaits us beyond the tomb. And yet perhaps even if he had spoken and his words had come down to us, we should not be much the wiser; for we have the testimony of St. Paul that it is idle to hope for an expression of the inexpressible: "Eye hath not seen, nor ear heard, neither hath it entered into the heart of a man . . ."[2]

But there is another question which vexes the mind; and to this we might well have expected an answer. What difference did his journey into eternity make to him — how did it

[1] John 11:39-44. The biblical references in these pages are based on the Douay-Rheims edition of the Old and New Testaments. Where appropriate, quotations have been cross-referenced with the differing names and enumeration in the Revised Standard Version, using the following symbol: (RSV =). — Ed.

[2] 1 Cor. 2:9.

alter his way of life when he returned to the world of time? Here, too, we are left baffled and without an answer; we are told nothing further of him at all, except that when, later on, Jesus went to Bethany and a supper was made for Him, Lazarus was one of the guests.[3] But what was he like? How was he changed? And perhaps, in default of information, we paint a picture of him for ourselves: we tend to think that with this unforgettable taste of infinity forever with him, he must necessarily have been dreamy, preoccupied, hopelessly bored with the unimportance, the pettiness, of the business of living, the everyday affairs of the world of men. You imagine the practical, motherly Martha having to tell him repeatedly at mealtimes: "Lazarus, do get on with your food."

Union with God increases zeal to do His work on earth

And yet there was a supper, and he was one of the guests. Was he, in fact, dreamy, abstracted, bored? Fortunately we need not be at a loss for an authentic answer; for if Lazarus himself does not supply one, there are plenty who do. There are plenty of others who, like him in what matters most, have known eternity and then returned to the world of time: there are all the saints who have been given in the heights of prayer knowledge of the secret things of God and in their ecstasy have forgotten everything but the Eternal, but who then returned again to the world of man.

And were they dreamy? Were they bored and preoccupied?

[3] John 12:1-2.

There was St. Paul who was rapt to the seventh Heaven;[4] and thereafter swept like a blazing fire through the length and breadth of the world. There was St. Teresa,[5] living with God in the heights of the prayer of union, yet always returning again to the busy, practical life of organization.

The list could be prolonged indefinitely. What is the explanation? Why is it that the picture we tend to paint for ourselves is so entirely at variance with the facts? For indeed we could surely appeal in support of it to common human experience: the man who has been through some intense experience does, in fact, tend to be preoccupied.

We shall find the answer in the most striking and explicit parallel to the experience of Lazarus: the story of St. Catherine of Siena.[6]

We are told that one day when her confessor was preaching a sermon in the church, they brought news to him that Catherine was dead. He went around to her house, where her followers were gathered weeping; but he, for his part, refused, in spite of the appearances, to believe that she was dead, and after a time she did indeed return to the world and open her eyes and become aware of what was going on around her. Now, her first words were much what we should have expected: for a long time she could only cry over and over again, "Oh, I am so unhappy," because she had seen the secret things of God and could not bear to be parted again from them. But that is not the whole story: far from it.

4 Cf. 2 Cor. 12:2.

5 Probably St. Teresa of Avila (1515-1582), Spanish Carmelite nun, mystic, and Doctor of the Church. — ED.

6 Dominican tertiary (c. 1347-1380).

For it was Catherine who, after this "mystical death," became one of the most famous and the most powerful women of her century, endlessly active, advising popes and princes, traveling, negotiating, issuing orders, determining policies, shaping the life of Christendom.

What had intervened? She had learned the truth expressed in the words of the pseudo-Denys:[7] *Omnium divinorum divinissimum est cooperare Deo in salutem animarum:* Of all divine things, the most divine is to share with God in the saving of souls.

She had begged our Lord in ecstasy to take her back to her eternal home, and she had been reproached by Him — for her *egoism*. She had been taught by Him: "You cannot render *me* any service, but you can help your neighbor. The soul in love with my truth gives herself no rest but searches ceaselessly to help others. You cannot give back to me myself the love I demand, but I have put you beside your neighbor so that you may do for him what you cannot do for me. What you do for your neighbor, then, I consider as being done for me."

And finally, there is the astonishing story of the exchange of hearts: the story that one day our Lord took her heart from her, and some days later gave her, instead, His own, so that from that time forward, she always prayed: "My Lord, I offer Thee *Thy* heart."

The substantial reality that we must see in this story, and apply to ourselves, is the fact that to have the heart of Christ means to be identified with the will of Christ: to will nothing that Christ does not will, to will everything that He does will.

7 Dionysius, the Pseudo-Areopagite (c. 500), mystical theologian.

And what is the supreme desire of the will of the Christ who is Lover and Savior, but to obey and glorify God by redeeming the world?

We must praise God in the things of the earth

Why, then, do we go wrong in our judgment about the saint returning from eternity into the world of time? Because we forget, or underestimate, the importance of the world. We forget, first of all, its importance as praising God. They tell us of another Dominican saint, Blessed Jordan of Saxony,[8] that one day as he was walking with some of his students along a country road, an ermine darted across into the hedge a few yards in front of them, and the youths, who had never seen one before, were disappointed at the short glimpse they had caught of it. Jordan went to the side of the road and called to the little animal to come out and let them have a look at it. It obeyed, put its front paws on his hand, and let itself be stroked. Then Jordan blessed it, and bade it go back and praise God.

The saints' lives are full of similar stories, because they remember the thing we forget: that the world is God's handiwork and His habitation, and that its destiny is to praise Him. "Bless the Lord, all ye works of the Lord":[9] the lilies of the field praise Him with their whiteness and the grass with its green; the birds of the air bless Him with the beauty of their flight; the beasts of the field bless Him in their work and their play. But these are not isolated voices raised to God; they are part

[8] Follower of St. Dominic (d. 1237).

[9] Cf. Daniel 3:57.

of the total song of the spheres, the song of all creation; for it is creation in its order and unity and wholeness which best reflects the beauty of God.

Man has, in this symphony of nature, a special, a directive, part to play: it is for him, first of all, to join in the song with immortal voice himself; but it is for him also to help with his husbandry the song of the lesser creation, and to raise it by his awareness and his loving worship of God to a more explicit sharing in the prayer of Christ — *instaurare omnia in Christo*.[10]

It is no mean thing, this song of the spheres, and the part which each creature plays in it: it was for this that the world was made. And when you return from prayer to the homely things of earthly life, it is this you must see in them; if you are tempted to be bored with them, remind yourself of this. You are called, with all the saints, to bless in the power of Christ's priesthood the song of the world, and to perfect it.

Love calls us to heal wounded creation

But there is much more than this. There is sin in the world. The song of creation is out of harmony: there are voices which are faulty or mute or discordant; the world of nature, as St. Paul reminds us, is still in travail, and the world of man is still sunk in sin and ignorance and malice. There is work to be done in the world by those who love God, redemptive work, and for that work, God *needs* them. The more you understand what this song of creation means, the more you will realize how imperfect sin has made it. But the more deeply you have

[10] "To re-establish all things in Christ"; Eph. 1:10.

become identified with the heart of Christ, the more you will want to help in redeeming creation and restoring the perfection of the song. And you can only redeem and restore in the degree to which, being first redeemed and restored yourself, you have learned to love.

Love of God requires death of self

Here is the clue to that paradox which runs right through the teaching of our Lord, the lives of the saints, and the sayings of the mystics. "Honor thy father and thy mother"; "by this shall all men know that you are my disciples, if you have love for one another"; "if any man come to me and hate not his father and mother and wife and children and brethren and sisters . . . he cannot be my disciple."[11]

How can we love and yet hate? How can we, with St. Paul, suffer "the loss of all things and count them but as dung," and yet, also with St. Paul, be "all things to all men"?[12]

St. Paul himself tells us how when he says, "I live, now not I, but Christ liveth in me."[13] St. Thomas Aquinas tells us how when, quoting the words of our Lord, he writes: "We must hate those near to us for God's sake, i.e., if they turn us away from God."[14] There is no answer other than an exchange of hearts with Christ; but in the exchange of hearts with Christ, there is an answer which is total, all-embracing, final.

[11] Exod. 20:12; John 13:35; Luke 14:26.

[12] Phil. 3:8; 1 Cor. 9:22.

[13] Gal. 2:20.

[14] St. Thomas Aquinas (Dominican philosopher, theologian, and Church Doctor; c. 1225-1274), *Summa Theologica,* II-II, Q. 26, art. 2.

You must give all to God; you must surrender everything; you must strip yourself of every vestige of self-will: it is the common teaching of all the saints and mystics. You must have no will in regard to created things but the will of God. You must enter into nothingness and, naked, follow the naked Christ.

But that does not mean that you may refuse creatures their rights, as things in themselves, as God's handiwork, and as part of the song of the spheres. It does not mean that you may shuffle off your responsibilities, that you may refuse to love what God loves. Jacques Maritain, in some magnificent and invaluable pages of *Les Degrés du Savoir,* has shown, first of all, the danger — a danger of total misunderstanding — which lies in confusing the language of mysticism with the language of theology; and secondly, the way in which theology can, in fact, state with perfect clarity the single truth in which the apparently opposing commands of love and hatred are made one. Noting that St. John of the Cross[15] bids his readers tear up by the very root all attachment to their families, Maritain asks this: "Are we to suppose that he is contradicting the common teaching of the Church, and notably of St. Thomas, on the love that is due to them? On the contrary, he is presupposing this teaching. He knows that his readers are no more likely to fall into insensibility than the contemplatives to whom he teaches the way of nothingness are likely to fall into quietism. . . . These prescriptions must be taken in all their force, without the least softening-down. But we have to understand them. They demand not only an external detachment

[15] Mystic and Church Doctor (1542-1591).

but an internal, radical, detachment, a complete death: but this means a radical renunciation of our *proprietorship* and *purely natural exercise* of our feelings, a renunciation thanks to which a greater love will vivify them. It does *not* mean a radical destruction of the (ontological) *reality*, if one may speak thus, of those feelings in themselves. Between these two sorts of death there is all the distance between the superhuman and the inhuman: as far as the growth in the life of the spirit is concerned, it is as great a disaster to abandon oneself to the second, and become hardshelled and cold of heart . . . as it is to reject the first, which means to refuse the perfection of love and the value to be set on it."[16]

The "expropriation of the self," dying, in the words of St. Bernard,[17] "the death of the angels": this is the meaning of all that the saints have to say of Christian detachment. St. John "preaches neither mutilation nor suicide, nor the slightest ontological destruction of the most fragmentary filament of the wing of the smallest gnat. He is not concerned with the structure of our substance and its faculties; he is concerned with our *proprietorship of ourselves*, as expressed in the use we make of our active power as free and morally responsible beings. And there he demands everything of us. There we have to give everything. What he does preach is a very real death, a death much more subtle and delicate than any material death or

[16] Cf. Jacques Maritain, *Les Degrés du Savoir* (Paris: Desclée de Brouwer et Cie, 1932), Annexe IX: *Les "Cautelas" de saint Jean de la Croix*. The English translation is *The Degrees of Knowledge* (New York: Charles Scribner's Sons, 1938, 1959). This appendix appears only in the 1959 edition, pages 468-470. — Ed.

[17] Abbot of Clairvaux and Church Doctor (1090-1153).

destruction: the death which is called the *expropriation of the self*. This destruction of self-will is a death which is active and effective within our being, a death which is experienced and freely undergone; it is within the innermost activity of the spirit that it takes place, and by the spirit that it is brought about. It grows with the growth of the spirit, and cleaves to it in its inmost depths. But it is a death which does not destroy sensitivity, but, on the contrary, refines it, and makes it more exquisite. It does not harden the fibers of the being, but, on the contrary, makes them supple, and spiritualizes them. It is a death which transforms us into love."[18]

Love of God calls us to love the world

And what follows? The more the saint burns out of his heart everything that savors of a proprietary attitude toward creatures (every vestige, therefore, of self-love) — in other words, the more he "despises creatures in the degree to which they are rivals to God or objects of a possible choice against God, the more he will cherish them in and for Him whom he loves, inasmuch as they are loved by Him. . . .

"For to love a being in and for God — I am speaking here of the love of friendship, not of the love of covetousness — is not to treat it as a pure means or occasion for loving God. That would mean excusing oneself from loving it in itself. And if we do that we cease immediately to love God truly, for we only truly love Him if we love also His visible images.

[18] Maritain, *The Degrees of Knowledge*, 407. (In this and the following quotations, I have made use of the English edition, but have departed from it a good deal in places.)

"No, to love a being in and for God is to love it in itself, and to treat it as an end, and to desire its good precisely because in itself and for itself it is worthy of love. . . . This is the explanation of the paradox whereby in the end the saint enfolds [everything] in a universal love of friendship and piety incomparably more carefree but also more tender and more happy than the possessive love of the voluptuary or the miser. [He enfolds in this love] everything which passes with time, all the weakness and the beauty of things, all that he has abandoned."[19]

But again what follows? We tend to think of wisdom as something wholly still, withdrawn, absorbed; but we are told in the Bible, on the contrary, that it is "more active than all active things."[20] We are here at the very keynote, on the practical side, of Christian contemplation. For it is through Christ that the Christian mystic comes to God; it is through Christ the Lover and Redeemer of men.

Having, through Christ, ascended to the Father, he cannot forget the suffering world which until the end of time is the preoccupation of the heart of Christ: "The grace itself which transforms us is the grace of our crucified Lord, and it is in order that we may share in the work that is His own, that is, to die for the world, that we are transfigured from brightness into brightness."[21]

So we find Catherine, her momentary egoism long outlived, longing to bear all the sorrows of the whole world on her

[19] Ibid., 411.

[20] Wisd. 7:24.

[21] Maritain, op. cit., 409.

shoulders; we find her, in fact, burdened with all the weight of the ship of the Church; we find her offering to Christ the heart of Christ, and therewith the love that was satisfied only when it broke upon the Cross.

So there are the two things, which are but two complementary aspects of a single life: there is the complete and utter dispossession of the self of all that is not God, so that in truth you can say, "I live, now not I, but Christ liveth in me" — the heart of Christ, the will of Christ, the power of Christ.

And there is at the same time what is precisely *implied* in those words: the fullness of love, the superabundance of life, the desire to work and suffer, even unto death, for the world that is loved with the love of Christ, a love which leaves nothing outside, a love for which nothing is too small, too poor, too weak, too full of sin.

We must love others with Christ's heart

Let us return to Catherine. The exchange of hearts is for her a beginning — it is what makes possible the immensity of her love and labors and power in the world. But it is also an end, a consummation. It is a consummation in the sense that it is the conclusion of a long and terrifyingly arduous process of expropriation of the self: to that aspect of it we must turn in a moment.

But it is a consummation also, and primarily, because it is in fact the very stuff of human destiny. "Seek ye first the kingdom of God":[22] we must not think of contemplation as a

[22] Matt. 6:33.

means to action, even the highest action; contemplation is not a means to an end, but is itself the end — an end so rich and full of superabundant life that, in fact, it is inevitably expressed in action as the vision of the artist or the lover is expressed in stone or paint, in word and gesture.

We shall never be saints if we ignore our responsibilities to the world, forget the law of love, close the bowels of our mercy against our brother, and try to build for ourselves a private and selfish beatitude. "By this shall men know that you are my disciples, if you have love for one another"; "if any man say: 'I love God,' and hateth his brother, he is a liar. For he that loveth not his brother whom he seeth, how can he love God whom he seeth not?"[23] And Ruysbroeck:[24] "Be kind, be kind, and you will be saints." Be kind: it is easy to be kind to our friends; but where shall we find the ability to be kind to *all*, to be kind to the people who irritate us, the people who attack and despise and malign us? We shall find it only in the heart of Christ.

And that is why, if it is a total misunderstanding of the Gospel to suppose that we are to seek our own sanctification, our own perfection, and ignore the needs of the world, ignore the very purpose of the human life of Christ, it is also a total misunderstanding to suppose that we can work for the world, as Christians, and so become saints, without being identified with Christ. "Unless the grain of wheat falling into the ground die, itself remaineth alone."[25]

[23] 1 John 4:20.

[24] Jan van Ruysbroeck (1293-1381), Flemish mystic.

[25] John 12:24-25 (RSV = John 12:24).

We must not wait until we are wholly transformed into Christ before attempting to share in His work in the world — if we did, we would have little to offer Him, most of us, when we died. It is a logical, not a temporal, order. But unless we try more and more, every day, to make our work in the world an expression of our love of God, unless we try to make every thought, desire, and action more and more completely identical with the mind and will of God, our work may remain our work instead of His, and then it will be of little value, and we may even commit the blasphemy of confusing end with means, and subordinating the love of God to the love of men.

We must desire only the will of God

The exchange of hearts is the consummation of a long and agonizing process: it is no easy thing to die and be reborn. There are many different kinds of saints: some we think of as fierce and some as gentle; some can find God only by withdrawing from the world to caves and desert places, and others find Him in the midst of men and in the voice of nature. But in one thing they are all equally fierce and equally unrelenting: in their struggle to expropriate the self, to kill the false self that wants to be its own master and refuses to be the child of God. This is a thing in which there can be no half-measures. It is the whole heart that has to be exchanged.

Sometimes there is an obvious and clear-cut choice to be made: I know that this is what I want, and that God's will is different; and you choose the will of God. That is something, but it is only a beginning. There are other choices to be made, when the thing you want is not wrong in itself and yet may not be God's will for you at this particular moment: and if you can school yourself to choose always the will of God in these things, that is something much more. But still it is only a beginning. You have not yet allowed the power of God to transform you wholly into Christ.

You must learn to be able to say *beforehand*, of whatever may befall, that your will is to do the will of Him who sent you into the world to praise Him. And you must learn to say it utterly and of everything. It means that there must be nothing, however small, or however good, to which you would cling for a moment against God's will: there is nothing about which you have not already said, "Thy will be done."[26]

That is the daily struggle and death of the Christian. There is no easy way.

In these days there is a growing interest in the way of the mystic, and let us thank God for it. But there is also a danger of being misled into supposing that to do as the mystics have done, it is sufficient merely to evolve a psychological technique — to learn the art of prayer without tears. There is no such thing.

It is not only the mind that has to be trained to see God. Blessed are the clean of *heart*. . . .[27] The power — let us make no mistake about it — comes only from God; and the power is offered. But to be able to accept it, we must have learned from God how to purify the will; we must have learned the lesson of detachment. We shall pray well only insofar as we become poor in spirit, meek, eager to suffer with Christ and for the sake

[26] Matt. 6:10.

[27] Matt. 5:8.

of Christ; only insofar as we can say in everything and about everything, "Thy will be done."

"Seek ye first the kingdom of God." That is the first lesson. If we learn that lesson, the rest will be added to us, will inevitably follow. But if we think we love God's creatures, but love them in defiance of God, we are not loving them; we are loving ourselves. Even though we give our bodies to be burned for them, we are not loving them; we are loving ourselves: because we are asserting that we know better than God what is for their good. The heart of man is not a house that can be emptied of one set of furnishings that another may be installed: it is not the *objects* of our love that have to be changed; it is our *love* that has to be changed by being transformed into the love which is the heart of Christ.

So we return to the practical hallmark of the Christian mystic: "By this shall men know that you are my disciples. . . ." The mysticism which seeks to advance by a purely human technique, relying on human powers, is in danger precisely of the disease of self-culture, of being turned in upon itself, of seeking ultimately only its own glory. But the grace which transforms the Christian "is the grace of our crucified Lord, and it is in order that we may share in the work that is His own . . . that we are transfigured from brightness into brightness."

Love of neighbor springs from love of God

The world has grown old and sterile because charity has grown cold. The love of men will grow weak and ineffective unless it is rooted in and expressive of the love of God; the love of God will also dwindle and decay into love of self unless it leads us to share in the redeeming activity of Christ. And perhaps it is true to say that outside the Church, that zeal for doing good in the world which is the glory of the West is losing its power because it is losing its roots in the love of God; whereas within the Church, on the contrary, the chief danger we have to fight against is the danger of a self-centered piety which neglects its duties to the world.

In the following pages, at any rate, it is the social implications of the Beatitudes[28] which have been mainly studied. But it is against the background of the love of God, above all and in all, that they must be seen.

For the Christian saint, love of the world does not make sense apart from love of God, precisely because it is wholly and entirely an expression of love of God. The will to work for the world does not make sense apart from the will of God, precisely because it is wholly and entirely a function of obedience to the will of God. If it is the reality of the world that we are discovering, it can only be because we are discovering the reality of God: if our hearts are growing to fullness of love for the world, it can only be because the false self is dying and we are being reborn in God.

We must be reborn to share in Christ's redemptive work

It is, then, that process of being reborn — the endless day-to-day struggle to find God, to come nearer to God, to

[28] The virtues that Christ preached in His Sermon on the Mount; see Matt. 5:3-9.

think and to will more and more exclusively as He thinks and wills — that is the *condition* of our sharing in Christ's redemptive work in the world. We shall totally misunderstand the Christian way of life if we suppose that that struggle can be put on one side while we attend only to the easier task of helping humanity.

It might be true to say, "Take care of contemplation — make sure it is fervent, assiduous, and wholly *God-centered* — and action will take care of itself; the redemptive work will inevitably follow in one form or another," but the reverse would certainly not be true.

What is the purpose of the grace of God, the sacramental system, the whole dynamism of the supernatural life, but to enable us to know God, to love God, to serve God? That is the "one thing necessary";[29] that is the only complete fulfillment of the heart's desire; and the fact that if we achieve it, we shall find much else included in it must not for a moment lead us into a confusion between the relative importance of finite and infinite.

In all that follows, then, these primary truths must be all the time presupposed and kept in mind. To be poor in spirit, to be meek, to be clean of heart: all these things denote an attitude of soul toward the world; but primarily they denote an attitude of soul toward God.

The Beatitudes mean, first of all, that the man who is poor in spirit and meek and clean of heart is succeeding in the essential Christian struggle and so is blessed: the struggle to kill the false self by the daily asceticism of accepting and

[29] Luke 10:42.

welcoming God's will, the struggle to find God by that daily searching and listening which is the life of prayer, the struggle with the mind's waywardness to gain, after immense difficulty and constant failure, that abiding sense of the presence of God, which is the condition of our ability to see and will all things in union with Him.

Yes, we must long and pray and work, to be filled with the love of our neighbor; but first of all, above all, we must long and pray and work to possess the one thing necessary, the substance of life everlasting, the thing whereof this other, when it is strongest and deepest, is the expression and the derivative: we must seek until we are given to find and possess, as Catherine did, the heart of Christ.

Chapter Two

The Beatitudes

God made us to know Him and to love Him and to serve Him, and so to be happy.

We should not be shy of the word *happy*. We have been given the gospel of life; we have been given the knowledge and love of Him who came that we might have life and have it more abundantly;[30] we have been given the freedom of the sons of God,[31] and although while we are on earth, it is not freedom from all misery, it is freedom from the deepest misery, and a prelude to the deepest happiness.

St. Thomas says, in a quiet, matter-of-fact way, that "happiness is the end of life";[32] there is no need to argue about that, only about how we are to find happiness. And that is what the Beatitudes tell us. To be suspicious of happiness and regard it as faintly irreligious is an unchristian thing — if you want to be a canonized saint, you must first become a notoriously happy person — but there are ways of searching for happiness

[30] John 10:10.

[31] Rom. 8:21.

[32] Cf. *Summa Theologica*, I-II, Q. 3, art. 1.

which are unchristian, too. The Beatitudes tell us how to be happy; and they tell us, all of them, that the way to be happy is to search for something else.

The Beatitudes show us how to attain happiness

If you want to be happy, then be poor in spirit, be meek, be clean of heart. These Beatitudes are not a question of virtue merely; St. Thomas gives us the clue to them all when he tells us that they are "certain excellent works of virtue under the impulse of the gifts of the Holy Spirit, whereby we approach the goal of eternal happiness, and have a foretaste of it even in this life." Happiness is not something to be searched for; still less is it something you can make; it is something you can only receive, and become.

There are two things to notice in this definition of the Beatitudes. In the first place, we are concerned with virtue in the Christian sense: virtue as determined by religion and built on humility and colored through and through by love. Because of all the labor involved in acquiring the habits of prudence, justice, and the rest, there is the same element of mastery, of the free, self-determining, independent personality, that you find in the picture of the virtues painted, let us say, by Aristotle; but that is only one aspect of Christian virtue. There is man the master; but there is also always the child. To say that the virtuous action is an act of religion is to say that your attitude must be primarily one of worship, your eyes fixed on God and not on yourself.

To say that love is the soul of all the virtues is to say that they are primarily a question not of doing but of being, of living in love, and that if they are not love-gifts, they are not really virtue at all. And then every virtue is a form of humility: prudence, the humility of the mind that can learn and that knows that wisdom must be wooed; justice, the humility of the man who knows that every possession is also a responsibility, to God and to the world, and that he is not the absolute possessor of anything, only its steward; temperateness, the humility of the flesh, the ability to reverence and not to maul; fortitude, the humble courage which says, "I can do all things" only "in Him who strengtheneth me."[33]

To obtain virtue, we must be childlike

To be humble and docile, to know the need of help and ask for it, and then to make both the asking and the acting an offering of worship and of love: this is the essential element in Christian virtue, because it preserves in the strength of the grown man the heart of the child.

But the Beatitudes tell us that, even so, virtue is not enough. The virtuous life is imperfect so long as we fail to be fully possessed of the virtues; and the remedy for that is plainly to grow in the virtues themselves. But the virtuous life is imperfect also because of the limitations of human virtue as such: when we speak of supernatural virtue, we mean the power of God active in the soul, but the use we make of the power is determined by human reason and circumscribed by its weakness; there is a lack of sureness of touch, and a niggling and pedestrian dependence upon rational argument, which

[33] Phil. 4:13.

you find gloriously superseded in the carefree spontaneity and uncalculating magnificence of gesture found in the saints. They have become, in truth, as little children, because they have learned how the human reason may be perfected by the divine: they have learned how to judge instinctively with the eyes of God by living in the life of God; they have learned that to be fully free, you must become wholly obedient to the touch of the Spirit.

Always, then, in the Christian life there are these two aspects, the man and the child; and it is the child aspect which makes virtue Christian, and which gives to the Christian who is possessed of it the freedom and gladness, the trustingness, the complete absence of self-righteousness and of calculating worry, and consequently the freshness and simplicity, that you find so prominent in the personality of the saint.

We must strive for both wisdom and simplicity

There are thus two dangers to be avoided. In the first place, there can be no deliberate cult of childish immaturity of mind and character. Yes, there is room in the Church for the "little ones,"[34] for those who are naturally simple, unlettered, uncritical; but there is no excuse for a deliberate stunting of the gifts of mind and character which God has given. You have to become a personality, to have a mind and will of your own; you have to learn to see and then to judge; you have to acquire the wisdom of the serpent as well as the simplicity of the dove.[35]

[34] Matt. 10:42.

[35] Matt. 10:16.

But then, in the second place, you have to preserve precisely that simplicity; you have to avoid the self-willed piety, the determination to decide at all costs for yourself what is right and wrong, the idea of the virtuous man as the self-made man, which will transform virtue from worship of God into something very much like worship of the self. You must be able to listen with childlike simplicity to the voice of God and to identify your own will with His; then you need the strength and maturity of the grown man in order to make your obedience to the voice not the obedience of a slave or an automaton, but the creative gift of a lover.

To learn to be fully man is hard, because it implies all the hardship of asceticism, the constant day-by-day struggle with what is weakly self-indulgent and disintegrating. But it is harder, perhaps, to learn to be reborn and to be a child: to learn first to see and love, to *receive* life from God instead of trying to make it for yourself, and so to be able to say, "I live, now not I, but Christ liveth in me."[36] Yet that is essential.

Christian virtue is a question not so much of doing as of being. When you hear it said of someone, "He's a different man since he fell in love," you have a clue to what must happen to the Christian. As you are, so you will act; love affects one's being, and therefore, in consequence, one's behavior: even though you do the same things, you will do them entirely differently — and it is when you can say, "I live, now not I" that you can go on to say "I can *do* all things"; and you can say the latter because you add, with the docility of the child, "in Him who strengtheneth me."

[36] Gal. 2:20.

We are made to live in oneness with all creation

Worship, then, is not a part of the Christian life: it *is* the Christian life. We shall be thinking, in some of these meditations, of the nature of sin: it is precisely the negation of the child. It is the attempt at autonomy — the desire to be self-sufficient, and to make the self the center of all things.[37] And in consequence, the wages of sin is loneliness, which is death.[38] For we are not made to be alone, but to live in the fullness of God's life and therefore in the warmth of God's family: it is sin that keeps us apart and closes our eyes.

First you must learn to see how your life is meant to be lived: in God, in oneness with all creation. All the things God has made are made ultimately of the same stuff, so there is a bond between them like the blood-tie that binds the members of a family; all the things God has made have ultimately the same end, to worship and praise Him in their different ways.

Most important of all, God Himself is present in all the things He has made, and His presence is discernible in them to the eyes of faith, love, and worship — and we best assist the song of creation, and recognize our oneness with all things most truly and fully, when we learn to see them in God and to see God in them; and then it is to Him that they can lead us.

[37] Children can, of course, in their own way, be extremely self-assertive: we are born in sin. The purpose of the contrast here made is not to idealize children in defiance of the facts, but simply to recall what our Lord tells us plainly: there is about childhood a quality which is too often lost in later life, but which we must recover by His grace if we are to be of His Kingdom. It is with this quality that we are here concerned.

[38] Rom. 6:23.

We must strive to participate in God's eternal present

But to see things thus is to see them not only in a new light but also in a new framework: the framework not of time but of eternity. We cannot escape from the former, but we can acquire the latter, the kingdom of Heaven.

For the pagan poet there must always be in his love of the beauty of things the sense of their transitoriness, the *lacrimae rerum*; for the Christian this is secondary. You cannot wholly escape the sadness of beauty's fading, the pain of loss or the pain of parting; but there is a sense in which nothing fades, nothing is lost, everything that is, is eternal, in the mind and heart of God. We mourn what is lost to us in the past; we long for what is not yet ours. But the life of God is not in time: in the life of God there is no past or future; there is only the eternal present. A fleeting moment of beauty is always equally present to God, whether it be for us in the long-distant past or yet to come in the remote future.

And so, to share in the life of God is, in a sense, to share in that permanence: it is to have, under all the pain that time inflicts, a deep sense of the abidingness of things, because it is to live, with God, in the eternal present.[39] So it is to be at peace, to have that peace which the world cannot give. To fall

[39] So the German mystic Blessed Henry Suso (c. 1295-1366), in his autobiography, writes of the detached man: "God has now become all things to him, and all things have become, as it were, God to him, for all things present themselves to him now in the manner in which they are in God, and yet they remain each one what it is in its natural essence." And later: "Be steadfast, and never rest content until thou hast obtained the now of eternity as thy present possession in this life, so far as this is possible to human infirmity."

in love is not primarily to *have* something new, but to *be* something new: this joy that I have, the actual presence, the sight and hearing, these can be taken from me; but if all of my love is part of my love of God, then the joy that I am — the joy that can become, as it were, a part of me — must abide, and distance cannot affect it.[40]

All this should give us a deep realization of the importance of each successive moment, since it is thus in this sense an eternal moment — an eternal act either of worship and gratitude and love or of selfishness and blindness. Forever and ever the priest and the Levite pass by the wounded man; forever and ever there is the glory of the love of the good Samaritan;[41] and every moment in our time-sequence must be either the one or the other.

The Beatitudes show us how to live

"Lord, that I may *see*!"[42] We have to know and love God before we can serve Him, with the service not of pride but of love. We have to learn to see and love the world of all created things as a family before we can treat it as a family. We have to learn to think of things not just as things that we *have* but as things that we *are*, if we live in love with them.

The Beatitudes tell us how to acquire this life, this more abundant life which it was Christ's mission to bring to us, this life of the man who is also a child, this human life which is also

[40] I have tried to deal more fully with this in *The Heart of Man* (NY: Longmans, Green, and Co., 1945), ch. 1.

[41] Luke 10:30-35.

[42] Luke 18:41.

the shared life of God. This life and power are offered; but we do not acquire them by passively waiting, but by the hard work of obedience and prayer. So, as we think over each of the Beatitudes in turn, we shall think also of the sacraments, which bring us the different kinds of energy that we need, and we shall think of the attitude required of us if the energy is to be used — an attitude expressed on the one hand by the gifts of the Holy Spirit and on the other by the various types of prayer.

"Send forth Thy Spirit, and they shall be created"[43] — re-created in the new life. That is the first thing we must think of: our need of the docility and the selflessness of the adoring child, rapt in God its Father. To live in the present is to live in the Presence: to see Him in all things and to see all things, all situations, all moments, all interests and desires, in Him. Sometimes we can persuade ourselves that we do this: we think we have given Him the whole of our lives, when in reality we are keeping some part of it locked away out of sight because we are afraid, because we know that until it is radically altered we can never see Him in it nor it in Him, and we resent the thought of His interference. But as we cannot say we love humanity so long as there are some who are our enemies, so we cannot say we love and worship God as we should until everything we do and are is an act of worship and everything we love we love in His presence.

God made us to know, love, and serve Him, and to be happy. The more you learn, by repentance and prayer and worship, to know Him, the more you will love; the more you

[43] Ps. 103:30 (RSV = Ps. 104:30).

love, the more you will want to serve; the more you serve, the more you will be happy.

If you learn to know the creatures of His hand, not just as things that you can have, but as part of the life that you are — the boundless life of love and worship of Him — then you will love them, too, aright, and you will want to serve them also. You will not be torn and disintegrated by clutching feverishly at the fleeting moment of time, but made whole by your vision of the manifold in the One, by your power to see and love all things in the peace of the abiding present.

And so your heart will be at rest because it will be filled with the all-inclusive Infinity for which it longs, and here and now you will be happy with the happiness of those of the kingdom of Heaven, for you will have been born again into the more abundant life, and that life will ceaselessly grow within you, until at the end, you are fully alive at last, and can fully and finally enter into the joy, the complete unshadowed beatitude, of the eternal day.

Chapter Three

Blessed are the poor in spirit, for theirs is the kingdom of Heaven.

Matt. 5:3

A. The Meaning of this Beatitude

Poverty of spirit

There is a sort of infinity in man, because of his power not only to become in a manner all things, but even, by the gift of God, to become one with the Maker of all things. To have our lives thus infinitely enlarged is to be happy; it is of this that the Beatitudes tell us. But we must start at the beginning.

They are grouped in an ascending order: not that as we progress from one to another, we leave behind us those that have gone before — all of them are always valid, always necessary — but that unless we can succeed in achieving the earlier, we shall never achieve the later. If we cannot be right in our attitude toward things, we shall never be right in our attitude toward anything.

Sin isolates us from God and creation

Man is made to be filled to infinity. But for that he must walk as a child with God; he must be able to receive His life; he must know and love and serve Him; and all this is made difficult, and without God's restoring power, impossible, because of the fact of sin.

Sin destroys the child. Instead of the docility which makes love and therefore oneness possible, there is the pride of attempted autonomy, the will to be one's own master, which is the state of isolation from God.

Isolation from God's family follows. For the proud man who sets out to be master of the world can never love the world; you have the kingdom not of the God of love but of mammon;[44] you have, not the oneness of knowing and loving and serving, but the chaos which follows from attempting to treat all things as your own creatures, as utilities merely, and to use all things, and animals and men and even God Himself, simply as means to your own profit or pleasure. So you have the man who possesses all things but has nothing; and he has nothing because he is alone, isolated from God, isolated even from God's creatures. What does it profit a man to gain the whole world and yet remain thus estranged, imprisoned, frozen in the husk of his own selfhood? To live the life of mammon is to be in Hell — for Hell, like Heaven, in the most important sense is not so much where you go as what you become; even in this life, it is to be bereft of God.

To be happy, we must be detached

The first step on the road to happiness is the escape from mammon. Happy are the poor in spirit. I lose God, I lose the world, and I lose myself, if I want only to clutch at things and use them for my own pleasure or profit. Therefore I must, through God's mercy, repent, turn back again, and be reborn.

[44] Cf. Matt. 6:24.

I must be "stripped of all things."[45] I must learn the lesson of detachment.

Detachment is both to care and not to care

Perhaps few things are more misunderstood than this idea of detachment. People sometimes think that it means not caring: it does, but, as we have seen, only if you add that it means caring, too. The detached man will care more for things than the avaricious and rapacious man; but he will care in a different way. He will not clutch and cling, in self-worship; his possessions, his desires, his attachments will not fetter his freedom and destroy his power of love, will not forever be an anxiety and an agitation of spirit. His is the prayer of the poet, "Teach us to care and not to care. Teach us to sit still."[46] And so he learns to be at peace.

Caring means treating all creation with reverence

The first thing is to care: it is precisely what the rapacious man does not do. We cannot help wanting things; it is our nature; but what makes the difference is how we want, and how we express our want. Things are not just means; they are God's handiwork, lovely in themselves, therefore, and to be treated with reverence. And they are one with us in the unity of God's family; and so they are to be treated with love. And they are His creatures and not ours, and so they are to be used

[45] Cf. Heb. 10:34.

[46] T. S. Eliot, "Ash Wednesday," Part 1.

or enjoyed — they are to become possessions — only within the framework of His will. You do no harm to God or to things or to yourself if you use them or enjoy them according to their nature and His will for you, provided your attitude is one of love and reverence, provided you have first learned to see and to love and to serve, provided you have learned to care.

We lose the power to love and enjoy things as we should when we lose the power of vision; and we lose the power of vision when we lose the life of the child. When the visionary gleam fades into the light of common day, we go on using things because we understand their utility, but more and more we forget that they are things in themselves, things of beauty; we forget to stop and look.

But that is just what we must learn again to do: to stop and look. We must learn to stop and look at all the things that God has made that come our way, and say, "How lovely you are"; but we must learn to say it as men living not in time only, but in the eternal present; not simply loving the things themselves, but with them praising the God of whom they tell, conscious of their abidingness in His unchanging eternity, and conscious, too, not only that their beauty is a reflection of His infinite Beauty, but that the invisible Beauty is within them and about them, hallowing them: *vere locus iste sanctus est*, truly this world is a holy place since the Holy has made it His home. It is that constant deep sense of the Presence that, if we can acquire it, will prevent our love of God's creatures from distracting us from God.

But we must learn, too, to see this inward beauty and holiness in the poor things, and the ugly, and in the things of mean repute, in the waifs and strays of the world, in the dull and colorless moments as well as in the moments of great joy. And we must learn to see each thing, each event, each fleeting moment, as forever abiding in the arms of God in the eternal present if we would learn to see them aright; for it is only thus that, to speak properly, we can learn to care.

We must love creation according to God's will

But then if you care like this, you learn also not to care. If you learn to see God in all things, you will learn to love them according to His will, not according to your own self-will. If you see things as in eternity, you are less a prey to the pain of their passing, and so you can learn more easily not to clutch at them as they pass. If you see God in all things and all things in God, you learn to be reverent and not proudly possessive. And where it is a question of legitimate possession and legitimate use — and these are measured by the end that God has set for you, your manner of life and the work you do and the needs of your being — then you will learn the more easily not to sin by excess or superfluity, nor to hold fast at all costs when God would take from you what He has given: you will learn the more easily not to care.

Poverty of spirit frees us from fear

Let us think a little of the ways in which this caring and not caring is to be expressed. There is, of course, to begin with, the vice of avarice: there is the desire simply to amass as much as one can for one's own ends, and to let nothing go. That way leads to complete slavery. But in smaller ways the same spirit can be discerned: the grudging lender, the man who covets and envies, the man who is proprietary about such things as he has, and ungenerous to the needs of others.

To be poor in spirit is to be large-hearted and openhanded; to be not too much exercised about legitimate worldly purposes; to be, on the contrary, carefree about success or failure, because whichever it is, it comes from God. To be poor in spirit is to have a childlike trust in Providence, and so to be freed from fear.

This freedom from fear is indeed the characteristic of those who have learned to care and not to care. To be grasping and possessive is to live always in anxiety and fear of loss; to live in the eternal present is to live in the love that drives out fear. Nothing can separate us from love if love is not what we have but what we are.

The poet's paradox ceases to be paradoxical if you see the different sense of the two words. Teach us to care: teach us the meaning of love. Teach us not to care: teach us not to worry; teach us to be free of the fetters of a false love, false precisely because it thinks of loving in terms of a fleeting possession instead of an abiding life and oneness.

St. Dominic[47] on his deathbed said to his followers, "Possess poverty." It is not, if you understand it and practice it aright, a privation, but a perfection, the perfection of freedom. It is not, if you understand it aright, a question primarily of much or little: quantity is determined by the end in view. It is a question less of what you possess than of how you possess it. The apostle must be free of possessions in the literal sense

[47] Founder of the Order of Friars Preachers (1170-1221).

because he must be free to be uprooted at a moment's notice at the call of his work: he must be able to travel light, and lightheartedly; it was that, no doubt, that St. Dominic had first in mind.

But the mere absence of chattels is not enough: you can be lacking in poverty of spirit if you possess nothing more than a cloak or a book; you can be poor even though you possess an empire if, while saying, "All things are mine," you add, "and I am Christ's, and Christ is God's."[48]

We are not owners, but stewards, of creation

Again, you can have few material possessions, perhaps none, and no avarice of mind about them, and still be lacking in poverty of spirit. You must be carefree about *everything* that you have, material or otherwise. All the gifts that God gives us are things for which we must care and yet not care; we are only stewards.

You have your own particular gifts and talents, of body and mind and heart: you must be openhanded with them, use them in your love and service of the world, and use them *as* God's gifts to you, so that you do not mind if what He has given He should take away: it is not your business; you are only a steward. You have the gifts He gives you to fill your heart and your worship of Him: the love He gives you for others, and the love He gives others for you; these, too, you must make part of your worship, and part of your love of His whole family: you are only a steward. You have the gifts He gives you of prayer

[48] Cf. 1 Cor. 3:22-23.

and virtue, the help He gives you to climb the scale of perfection: and here, too, you must not grasp and worry and keep your eyes fixed always on yourself; you must do what you can at the present moment to make of these gifts a more perfect worship, leaving to Him the question of progress or failure: you are only a steward.

You are only a steward of all that you have and all that you are; a steward for God and for His family. But you are meant to be more than stewards of God's things: you are meant to be lovers as well. If you hurt anything of the things that God has made — by lust or tyranny or blindness or by using things in any way as mere means to your pleasure or profit — you hurt yourself and all the world, because to that extent you continue to destroy the unity of the family. But if you love, and therefore can serve as well as use, can reverence as well as master; if you are a contemplative and have learned to see and love instead of grabbing; and if your love is worship of God and not of yourself, if your love is as deep as the sea but as carefree as the wind, then you return to the integrity of God's family, and, having nothing, you are at peace, because you have nothing to lose, and at the same time you possess all things, for yours is the kingdom.

Only Heaven fulfills our deepest desire

Yours is the kingdom of Heaven: even in this life it can be true. The desire to have lies deep in us — we are indeed compact of desire — but it is a desire for infinity, which the gaining of the whole world will not fulfill. The desire to have is deep in us: but it is really a misunderstanding if we think of it thus instead of as a desire to *be*. The heart is an infinite capacity and thirst for *being:* and we are never at rest until it is filled. And so we try to fill it by drawing many things toward us and making them ours, until the house is cluttered with furniture, and we cannot move, and still we are tormented. Blessed are the poor in spirit because they have seen that this is not the way, and have known that an infinity not of having but of being is the kingdom.

See the immensity, even in this life, of the saints who, having nothing — having no riches, no worldly power or influence — can yet draw all things to them, not by force or fear but in love and homage, and so are filled: theirs is the kingdom which has no boundaries; theirs is the earth and sky and stars, and, still more, the uncharted splendors of the light inaccessible. For they have learned what Mary learned, and have chosen with her the better part; and it shall not be taken from them.[49]

[49] Luke 10:42.

B. *The Gift of this Beatitude*

Devotion and the gift of fear

You shall know the truth: and the truth shall make you free. . . . I will not now call you servants . . . but I have called you friends. You are my friends if you do the things that I command you.[50]

If you are poor in spirit, you learn not to care, in the sense of not endlessly fretting and worrying, even about your own state of soul.

We, in this country and century, are perhaps inclined to take too negative a view of morality: to think it means just not doing things which are forbidden. "Nanny, go and see what Richard is doing, and tell him to stop it": that is the voice of morality as we sometimes conceive it; but it is not the voice of Christian morality.

Morality for the Christian is religion; and religion is love; and love is not a negative but a creative thing. To know and love and serve: the moral life is a question first of what we ought to be, and only then, in consequence, of what we ought to do — and only thirdly, by implication, of what we ought not to do.

[50] John 8:32; 15:15, 14.

Servile fear is the least motive for morality

The negative attitude of mind leads us away from the religion of love to the religion of servile fear. What a terrible thing it is to teach the young that being a good Catholic simply means avoiding doing certain things, and that if they fail to avoid these things, God will see them and will visit His anger on them.

What a different story the Gospels have to tell us. God is love: so how can we depict Him as a sort of omniscient policeman? There is punishment, yes; but not arbitrary punishment: if I act thus, I make myself thus; and to be thus is itself a misery, a punishment. We cannot fall into grave sin unawares; we can only go to Hell if we choose deliberately to love evil instead of God, and therefore become incapable of living any life but the life of isolation from God, the life of Hell.

God is terrible, yes; He is also lovely. You cannot think of Him aright unless you have both of these qualities in mind. There are times when we have to think of the terror and the punishment in order to keep ourselves from disaster; but that means that love and therefore religion are at a low ebb within us. Servile fear is the lowest motive; there are better ways of keeping the commandments than that.

You could think of them as what, in fact, they are: the pattern you have to follow if you want to be whole and happy, a complete human being: that is better than the morality of the slave. You could think of them also as God's will, the will of His love, and therefore as religion, as your worship of Him: the result of living in love, in the eternal present; and this is the Christian way in its fullness, because in this way you have made your will identical with God's will, and so you are become one with Him.

Childlike fear must mature into loving awe

But although this oneness is far from the religion of servile fear, fear of another sort is still an essential element in it. Fear is the beginning of wisdom: without fear we cannot be taught, we cannot grow; but it is not present only at the beginning.

Beyond the completely servile fear of the slave, there is the fear of the loving but as yet unreasoning child, and its fear is an element we cannot ignore or try to eliminate, although if we teach and train aright, it will pass as the child grows in grace and wisdom into the higher, freer and reasoned obedience of the son, in which it becomes mainly or exclusively reverential. Beyond this again there is the fear, wholly identified now with loving awe, which is proper to the lover.

The life of the spirit must follow these progressive steps from fear to fear. We shall never learn to love God aright unless we have learned to sense His majesty, to know Him as terrible. But that same sense of awe is never left behind: it grows as wisdom grows. For it is simply the recognition of the abyss which lies between creature and Creator; and it must grow in intensity as we come to realize more fully what *infinity* means. This fear, which is not only compatible with, but an essential element in, our divine sonship, is the *condition* of love as of wisdom; for it is what makes us teachable; and so we have to guard it and labor to deepen and intensify it, until it can become, in the end, a part of Heaven's unending hymn of praise and glory.

Children must be taught to love and serve

Surely it is this idea of reverential awe as an element in the religion of love that we should teach the young, and not the negative religion of fear alone. But if we are to avoid this unchristian cult of negative fear, it will mean that although, of course, the whole of school life must be presented as part of religion, religious practice itself will be as far as possible differentiated from ordinary school discipline and its sanctions; it will mean, too, a very clear distinction between giving guidance and encouragement on the one hand — little children need to be led by the hand to prayer and confession and so on — and anything like enforced piety or dragooning on the other.

It means that although you can no doubt preserve them for a time from doing wrong by treating them like hothouse plants, guarding them from the knowledge of evil, keeping them in negative innocence, you will not do so: you will not purchase innocence at the price of ignorance and lack of self-reliance. You will want them to know and love and serve God, and so you will teach them the lessons of freedom and responsibility: you will teach them, not to avoid danger at all costs, but to be strong enough to meet and conquer danger: you will teach them, not to want above all to be safe, but to want above all to love and serve.

Holy fear is necessary

God is terrible; we cease to be religious at all if we forget that and turn Him into a mascot. To grow in wisdom and love is not to lose all fear of God; it is to change our fear of God. It is to pass from the servile fear of the slave, the fear of punishment, to the loving reverence of the son, fearing to offend his father, and, in the end, to the purely selfless fear of the lover, the fear of hurting what you love. That fear, *reverentia*, remains even in Heaven; for it is an essential element in love, in the child-vision; it is also an essential element in art. Without it you can never learn to know and to love; neither can you learn the art of serving God and the world.

But we misunderstand this fear completely if we think of it as endless agitation, anxiety, and fright. "Fear not,"[51] our Lord says again and again in the Gospels; and if you are poor in spirit, how can you fear, since you put all that you have and all that you are into God's hands, secure in trust? If you are filled with the caring which is love and emptied of the care which is worry, then necessarily you are filled with the fear which is awe, but emptied of the fear which is anxiety and fright.

Negative fear leads to scruples

Do not worry. There is a danger for us, in the West, with our Latin heritage of logic and law, of falling prey to the disease of scrupulosity, a disease for which the Eastern Church, with its emphasis on grace and freedom, has no name. We must not attempt to lessen our respect for our heritage on this account; on the contrary; but we must make sure that we are learning to see and love the law of God in terms of the life of God, and the clear-cut definitions and directives of ethics in terms of the freedom of the sons of God.

[51] Matt. 10:31; Luke 12:7, 32.

Our Lord came primarily, not to bring us an ethical code, but to bring us life. We cannot have too delicate and reverent an obedience to His will; and at the beginning we necessarily find that we have to force ourselves to obey, and that our motive is often the motive of fear rather than of selfless love; but unless we are trying to turn our obedience, slowly and gradually, into the obedience of love and therefore of free choice, we may find ourselves being swamped by negations, a prey to fears and scruples, and in the end become victims of that self-centeredness which it is the precise purpose of the Christ-life within us to uproot.

Do not worry. You have to make your examination of conscience, for example. But let it not be anxious, meticulous, and wholly negative; instead let it be sane, brief, and positive, the eye always on love, for it is by love that we shall be judged in the end.

Do not worry. You have, or will have, your real problems to face: and you must face them squarely, think them out as best you can, pray and take advice, docile to God and His representatives; but then, when a decision is reached, you must rest in God, leave it to Him, refuse to keep going over and over the same ground, refuse to become introspective, and set yourself, instead, to the positive tasks of life, be outward-turning in love of God and His family, be active and creative in the work He has given you to do.

Awe should be the foundation of our prayer

Be outward-turning: it is the only way to escape from the bondage of the original sin of self-worship. But we must be outward-turning first of all to God.[52] And what is the first Godward step, the first step in the life of prayer? Surely we do well to remember that here, too, "fear is the beginning of wisdom,"[53] and that our prayer will be sound and humble and fruitful if it is built on the foundation of awe.

The first prayer is the prayer of awe of the Unknown, the prayer of the little child in the face of mystery and infinity, the prayer of Thomas the Apostle abashed by the response to his lack of faith: "My Lord and my God."[54] That is the first prayer; God can begin to do something with us then. We are taught to say "Our Father";[55] we are told that we are God's family; but we must have not the proud familiarity which is a form of contempt but the humble familiarity of the child. Perhaps to achieve it we need a deep sense of sin; certainly we shall never have it until we are possessed by a sense of the distance between the Perfect and the imperfect, the Creator and the creature, between Being and nothingness; we shall never have it until we can pray the prayer of awe.

But if we can so pray, acknowledging fully the authority and the majesty as well as the nearness of God's fatherhood,

[52] To be outward-turning in this sense means that we fix our eyes on something other than our own self; we cease to be self-centered. It does not mean an absence of recollection; it does not mean anything other than St. Augustine (Bishop of Hippo and Doctor of the Church; 354-430) meant when he told us, "*Noli foras ire*" — do not go out beyond the mind, for God is within the mind. These spatial metaphors must be used with caution: the one essential thing, quite simply, is that we should look at God, not forever at ourselves.

[53] Ps. 110:10 (RSV = Ps. 111:10).

[54] John 20:28.

[55] Matt. 6:9.

acknowledging the abyss into which our sin has plunged us, and looking in sorrow and humility to God for our deliverance, then we can indeed become His sons, and coheirs with Christ, and so be free and happy and at peace.

Fear of the Lord is the beginning of wisdom

And what is the gift which can teach us all this? Fear of the Lord is the beginning of wisdom: we keep our lives and our conduct worshipful first of all by obeying the impulse of the Holy Spirit through the gift of fear; for so we begin to turn our backs on what is self-willed and self-determined; we begin to acknowledge the divine fatherhood in all that we are and do; we learn to be docile; we learn to be born again as little children, and so to become truly wise.

The gifts are all forms of docility to the Holy Spirit; but the gift of fear is the first gift in ascending order precisely because fear is the first stage in complete docility to the impulses of the Spirit, and therefore it is what makes it possible for the Spirit to perfect us wholly through the other gifts; it is the gift of fear, just as it is that poverty of spirit which is the corresponding beatitude, which begins in us the reversal of pride and self-will; it is fear and poverty of spirit alike which teach us to pray the prayer of awe, and so to begin our life where it must be begun, in an attitude of reverent adoration of God.

To be filled with poverty of spirit and with this fear which is not only compatible with love but grows stronger and deeper with the growth of love: this is to become free of the religion of negations and to begin the life of devotion, the life in which morality is transformed into worship by the alchemy of love.

Devotion is not the same as pious feelings

The word *devotion*, in its turn, is sadly misunderstood in these days. Essentially it has nothing whatever to do with emotion: it is not a question of feeling good. You can be filled with devotion and yet experience nothing but aridity, even an agony of boredom, in prayer. This identification of a loving state of soul with pleasant feelings is very dangerous: you may think you are worshipping God when in reality you are indulging your own desire for a sense of security, your desire to be comfortable and at rest.

There are times when God makes the life of prayer very pleasant to His servants; that is His affair, not theirs. The testing time — and the time, therefore, when fidelity to prayer and the life of virtue is most valuable — is the time when nothing is made easy for us, and when we cling on, if at all, only by sheer strength of will. It is just this, the will, that is the essence of devotion: "the will," St. Thomas tells us, "to give oneself readily to the things which concern the worship of God."[56]

And love, he tells us, is what causes devotion, because it is love that makes us eager to serve the one we love; while on the other hand it is devotion that nourishes love because love is safeguarded and increased by loving deeds, which are the expression of the loving will.

And what is it in terms of prayer that causes devotion? It is filling the mind with the thought of God's goodness and man's helplessness: of God's goodness, because this thought brings

[56] Cf. *Summa Theologica*, II-II, Q. 82, art. 1.

forth love in us; and of our own helplessness, because this excludes presumption, and brings us back again to the humble docility of the child.

The prayer of awe helps us restore the world

"My Lord and my God." The prayer of awe can do two things for us. In the first place, it will lay the foundations for our own lives. Learn to live habitually in the thought of the omnipresent majesty of God, the immanent Transcendent; learn to realize habitually that all you see and touch and handle is God's handiwork and still more the habitation of His glory; learn to see every event and action in the light of the eternal present, and every decision you have to make as a decision of love, and the whole tissue of your life as a single prolonged act of worship; learn to say "Our Father" with the thought in your mind that you are a son indeed, but a prodigal son; and then you will be humble and poor in spirit, and be living in the kingdom.

There is the second thing that the gift of fear will do for us. We are all together God's family; you cannot think of your life apart from the lives of these your brothers and sisters. The gift of fear and the prayer of awe have their social purpose, too. They will help to restore a world living more and more on the surface of life: you must pray, and pray this prayer of awe, to give back the dimension of *depth* to life on earth. William Law[57] speaks of those who try to escape from the terrifying reality of God by seeking refuge in the externals of religion: it

[57] English spiritual writer (1686-1761).

is only one stage better than trying to forget reality by the endless pursuit of pleasure.

Pray the prayer of awe, and live in docility to the Spirit's gift of loving reverence, and then you will worship in spirit and in truth and help to restore the world to the wholeness of the life of worship: you will help to teach a world which is proud and uncaring in its belief in its own maturity and its own self-sufficiency that there is no real life, and therefore no real happiness, except in poverty of spirit, except in the infinite life of God: and you will teach all this by being yourself a child, for of such is the kingdom of Heaven.[58]

[58] Mark 10:14; Luke 18:16.

C. The Sacrament of this Beatitude

Baptism

Amen, amen I say to thee, unless a man be born again of water and the Spirit, he cannot enter into the kingdom of God.[59]

The gospel of our Lord Jesus Christ is the gospel of life: He came that we might have life, and have it more abundantly. That life and that power are in the world; and the sacraments were instituted by Christ as the normal way in which that life and that power might be poured into our souls. That is why they correspond to all the great crises or turning points or major needs of life: birth, adolescence, nourishment, marriage (or the special vocation of the priesthood), sickness, and death.

They make use of material things — water, oil, bread — because we are not pure spirit but body-spirit, and because, not spirit only, but the whole material universe needs the restoring power of Christ. They make use of material things also because of the power of material things to speak to the mind and heart of man through symbol — and we might think and study and

[59] John 3:5.

pray a long time before coming to the end of the riches of the Church's symbolism.

In Baptism, we receive new life and truth

The first sacrament is the sacrament of rebirth: specifically the freeing of man from the bondage of the evil power, the mystery of iniquity in the world, and his rebirth into the kingdom as a child of God, filled, therefore, with the power of God, the power to be good and to do good in the world.

Baptism uses the symbolism of water, and in it you have the two things: the cleansing and the life-giving qualities. "Go forth, unclean spirit," the priest commands: that is the first thing, the liberation from the power of evil. "And give place to the Holy Spirit coming down from Heaven": that is the second, the new life. Let us think what exactly this new life means.

First of all, you are given truth, wisdom; you are given what we call the Faith. It is not just a series of disconnected statements, to which you are asked to give your assent; it is not only a coherent system of truths about God, so that you know with some accuracy whom and what you are to worship; it is a view of God which essentially implies and teaches a coherent view of life and the world as a whole: you have the key which can unify all your acquired experience and learning, and give a unified direction to all your desires and ambitions.

Our civilization tried in the past to order its life and arrange its world-view without reference to God: it wanted to be just human, and to have just a human universe; and now that we are reaping the results, we know how miserably it failed. It could not do otherwise. We cannot be just human: we must either accept the gift of God and be more than human, or reject it and become less than human.

But if you have the Faith, then you have, first of all, a view of reality which is inclusive, and therefore gives the ultimate answer to the questionings and searchings of the mind: there is nothing too big to become part of it. It satisfies the mind because it enables the mind to see the manifold in terms of the One, which is the perennial need and desire of mind as such.

But it is not just an abstract knowledge of truth that is given in the sacrament of Baptism: it is the abiding *presence* of the Truth. God is with us, and in us. And to be faithful to the Faith is, therefore, to live always in that presence, and to find in it both the motive force and the standard of judgment for all life and all action.

Baptism gives not only truth to the mind, but power to the will. It is a power that must be translated into facility by long and arduous practice, certainly; when we speak of infused virtues, we do not mean that we shall begin, as though by magic, to act always and effortlessly in a virtuous way. But we do mean that we are no longer inevitably bound by the bondage of evil to work evil in the world: the seeds of the new life are within us.[60]

[60] It is important to make it clear that when we think thus of the power of Baptism to bring forth the new life in the Christian, we are not presuming to limit the power of God in any way: the sacraments are the *normal* means, not the only means; there is the baptism of desire, and it is the traditional doctrine of the Church that God does not deny His life and power to any who strive equivalently to worship and serve Him according to the light He has given them: it is not for us to attempt to assess their numbers.

What is essentially given is thus the power of entering into the kingdom, the power of Heaven. When the human being is thus filled with the life of God, he has within him precisely the life which is Heaven, although he has it only in germ: and all that he does, his thought and willing and prayer and action, can increase that life within him and make him more and more heavenly in himself.

Baptism allows us to see God's presence on earth

Baptism gives us also a new earth; but that is not the thing of first importance. There is no doubt about the mind of Christ here as the Gospels reveal it: the water in the well at Sichar is good and necessary, but not so necessary as the waters of life;[61] the wedding and the wine at Cana are good, but the following scene in the Temple shows us that we must not think the service of God can be subordinated to worldly purposes.[62] If we seek first the kingdom of God and His justice, the new earth will be added to us; if we give the earth and its fullness pride of place in our lives and our hearts, we are idolaters, and turn the house of God into a den of thieves.[63]

But it remains true that to live the life of God *is*, in fact, to find a new earth, to see the earth as the habitation of His glory, to see all things in Him and Him in all things. We know the power that things have to hurt us or give us joy because of their association with people we love: you love this place because

[61] John 4:5-7, 10; Rev. 21:6.
[62] John 2:1-10, 14-16.
[63] Matt. 21:13.

one you love made it Heaven for you; you cannot go into this room without pain because one you love once lived in it. To the eye of faith, all the things that God has made have this richness of association, and it should always be a cause for rejoicing, because the presence within them is an abiding presence and glory. The pagan *lacrimae rerum*, the pathos of the passing of earthly beauty, is far from being the final word: in the eternal present all things abide, and behind the gleam of created beauty you sense the splendor of the divine. *Vere locus iste sanctum est:* "truly this place is holy" . . . the house of God and the gate of Heaven.

The power of Baptism transforms the world

But Baptism affects more than our way of *seeing* the world; it gives us not just a new vision of the earth but a new earth. We must see the power of the sacrament in the context of the mystery of iniquity as a whole: the entrance of the power of good into a world given over to the power of evil.

This is not simply an affair of the individual soul: it has always its cosmic significance. Think of the history of the world as the history of the struggle between good and evil, the might of God and the might of the rebellious spirit; think of the world as the battleground on which the struggle is waged, and the souls of men as either in bondage to fight on the side of evil or freed to the service of the Light; think of the world of nature as involved in the grip of evil on the universe, and therefore as needing, in degree, the healing and restoring power of the Spirit: and then you will see the significance of Baptism for the world as a whole.

All that sense, which you find so strongly marked in the early Church, of the power of the God-life in man to heal sickness and suffering and to tame the wild brutality of created things, the power to restore and heal the world by goodness and love, is simply an affirmation of the importance of Baptism for the world as a whole.

True, the power it gives is primarily a passive power, the power to be a child of God; but that power itself creates a responsibility. You were a slave, now you are free; and therefore you have the responsibility of the free man. You are responsible for your family. You are to share in Christ's healing work: first, of course, for the sin of the world, but then also for its suffering. To be freed from evil is not only to be "made whiter than snow";[64] it is to become white with the whiteness of white-hot fire, to be on fire to heal and to help. Every Christian is meant to be, in Christ, a mediator.

We are called to make truth part of our very being

But we shall not mediate as we should, we shall not spread the light in the world, unless we have ourselves first seen the light truly, learned the true Faith and not a travesty of the Faith. We believe not in propositions but in the reality which is expressed by the propositions; we believe not in a creed but through a creed.

The expression of divine reality in human words is necessarily inadequate; the understanding of the divine reality by the human mind is necessarily groping, and we may well make

[64] Ps. 50:9 (RSV = Ps. 51:7).

mistakes. It is possible to accept the formulas of the creeds and still to have a quite wrong idea of the nature of God and of His Providence; it is possible to worship God and still to fall into a sort of practical idolatry.

If you turn your religion into magic, if you expect an immediate and literal answer to all your prayers, if you expect the grace of God to do for you by miracle what only demands a little hard work, you are misunderstanding the Faith.

If you think of God in such a way as to project onto Him the human emotions of jealousy, anger, and spite, you are misunderstanding the Faith. If you turn your worship into self-indulgence, your progress in virtue into self-glorification or spiritual valetudinarianism, or your religion into a purely formal and external affair, then you are misunderstanding your Faith.

If you allow yourself to accept the assumptions of a pagan environment as far as conduct is concerned, and keep your Faith in abstraction from practical affairs, you are betraying it. And you are betraying it, too, if you think of it simply as something received from without, a static deposit, which you have only to accept and guard but without making it your own, without *becoming* it.

The truth is given us from without, yes; but it is something that we have to realize in actual experience: we have to translate the formulas of the creed into the stuff of life; we have to learn so to see the Faith in all the everyday circumstances and events of life that it becomes not something we sometimes think of but something we always are. We shall not mediate as we should, we shall not spread the light in the world, unless we see the light truly, as it is.

But we shall not mediate as we should, we shall not spread the *power* in the world, unless we are sufficiently docile and humble to receive the truth not with the reason only but with the depths of the spirit, and so to become really the instruments of God in and for the world.

The Christian is a mediator inasmuch as, being one with God, he is also one with his fellowmen, and lives to serve them, to pass on to them the God-life that is in him: but for that, you must be faithful always to the presence, you must be poor in spirit, you must have learned to pray the prayer of awe. Then you will *be* the sort of person who will influence the world, not necessarily by doing much, but simply by being what you are.

Poverty of spirit brings us joy

That should be the effect of Baptism in us: to give us the eternal present beneath and beyond the fleeting world of time, to teach us to live in the Presence, and thus to be at peace; to teach us to say, "I live, now not I, but Christ liveth in me," and thus to put all things into His keeping. If at long last we can succeed in doing that, we shall know the freedom of the sons of God, the carefree peace that follows upon poverty of spirit and upon the docility of the gift of fear: we shall be glad because we shall not be solicitous, not be grasping, not be self-willed; we shall be glad because we shall be openhearted and openhanded, for we shall know, in the depths of our hearts, that what we are and have is not ours but God's, and we shall be happy to know it; we shall be glad with all the new-found gaiety of the child reborn within us, the child who has everything to enjoy and love and nothing to lose; we shall be glad because we shall know that we are no longer in the darkness, that spring has replaced the spirit's winter, the "rains are over and gone,"[65] and that if we are faithful, we can live not only now but forever and ever in the Light that is Life everlasting.

[65] Song of Sol. 2:11.

Chapter Four

Blessed are the meek, for they shall possess the land.

Matt. 5:4

A. The Meaning of this Beatitude

Meekness

Some people suppose that to have dominion over great riches and possessions, material and otherwise, is the key to happiness. Our Lord tells them that they are wrong, and that, on the contrary, they must be poor in spirit if they want to be happy.

Others suppose that they will be happy if they can dominate their environment, if they are men of power and fulfill their aggressive instinct by expressing to the full what the Bible calls the pride of life.[66] Our Lord tells them that they, too, are wrong, and that to be happy, they must learn to be meek.

The second beatitude builds on the first. You could be poor and still not happy, because you could be poor not from love but from pride, from the arrogance which refuses to share in the blessings of the common herd. Your poverty must go with humility and piety; St. Thomas connects this beatitude, as we shall see, with the gift of piety, for it is the outcome precisely of the sense of our own creatureliness and dependence on God, and in particular of our need of a savior to free us from the bondage of evil.

[66] 1 John 2:16.

To find God, we must die to ourselves

There is surely a connection between the superficiality and the arrogance of much of our modern manner of life and thought, and the decay in our times of the sense of sin. We like to think that human nature is capable, of itself, of dealing with the problems which confront it, and of securing its own happiness. And so we fight shy of the deep places with which we cannot in fact deal; and perhaps we pretend that the deepest problems do not really exist at all. But if we live on the surface of life, we miss the meaning of life. There is only one way to know reality fully, and to live fully: we have to die and be reborn.

If you study the mythologies and folklore of the peoples of the world — those legends which are either the distorted echoes of primitive revelation or the natural expression of the deepest desires of the heart of man, or both — you find the same theme constantly recurring: the hero must make his long journey through the darkness of the sea or the night; he must slay the dragon or the serpent; and he must come through death to the new life, the new birth.

In the Christian story, which is the fulfillment of these secular dreams of humanity — because, in it, dream and actual destiny are one — you find the same theme in its highest form in the sacrificial death of the Word who was made flesh and dwelt among us that we might be reborn to be sons of God.[67]

But this is not simply a vicarious redemption in which we have no part: what was done in and by Christ must be done

[67] John 1:14, 12.

also in a different fashion in and by ourselves; in us, too, the dragon must be slain, and we, too, must pass through death to the new life. What is the dragon? The power of evil, the mystery of iniquity, whose bondage we are under as long as we are living not in God but in sin. And what is the death? The death of the false self: the self set up in rebellion against God, the self which seeks to be self-sufficient. How then are we to be reborn and become whole? By finding our true center, which is God, by finding God in all things, and the desire of God in all desires, and thus by beginning to live the life of worship instead of the life of self-worship.

But this in its turn implies a precedent turning away from the false self, an acknowledgment of our essential insufficiency. And it means, because of our state of sin, an acknowledgment of our need of a savior without whom we cannot, in our bondage, turn away from ourselves.

We find God by making for ourselves the long sea-journey, in the company and in the power of Him who made it for us first; we find God by overcoming, again in His power, the dark evil within us; we find God by realizing in the first place our need of God, as a child realizes his need of a father; we find Him by learning to see the reality of sin and therefore to repent and to be meek and humble of heart.

We must recognize evil to overcome it

"He descended into hell."[68] That, too, we have to do in company with Him. Together we are all God's family, and we

[68] Apostles' Creed; cf. Eph. 4:9.

have to go down into the depths and understand the reality of the evil of the world if we are to help heal the world. You cannot heal unless you love, but you cannot love unless you see.

That is why the first prayer of the humble man is the prayer of the blind man in the Gospel: "Lord, that I may see."[69] Lord, that I may see the reality of sin and my share in it, and so turn again to You, and so see Your mercy and the meaning of the Love that rules the sun and the other stars. For then the Word will be made flesh in me, and I shall be reborn, and in the power of the new life, I shall share in the work of Him who makes all things new.[70]

You cannot help the world in its sin and its suffering unless you sense your share in the sin and have your share in the suffering. And how can you do this, not only for a few who are dear to you and for whom you are responsible, but for the whole world? You can do it only by putting on Christ, by being able to say, "I live, now not I, but Christ liveth in me." And who can begin to say this but the meek and the humble of heart? For the proud man lives aloof, and in isolation, never in oneness with the Life. If you are humble enough to put on Christ, then you can live and work in the power of Christ and according to the will of Christ: you begin gradually to become, in the words of St. Gregory Nazianzen[71] describing the effect of the Spirit's gifts, *organum pulsatum a Spiritu sancto*, an organ played on by the Holy Spirit: you begin to have the obedience and docility to use all your energy in the service,

69 Luke 18:41.

70 Rev. 21:5.

71 Bishop of Constantinople and Doctor of the Church; called "the Theologian" (329-389).

not of selfishness, but of the Other; to sow, and to leave the reaping to God; to live in the present, and leave the future issue to His good pleasure.

Meekness requires obedience

To be meek, then, is first of all to be obedient — to be obedient, as far as you can, with the loving obedience which is the expression of an identity of a deep personal will like that between lovers. That is the obedience which is the highest form of freedom, the freedom of the sons of God; and it is thus that we should think of our obedience to the Church, to our vocation, to our conscience: an obedience which sometimes implies a struggle within the mind, sometimes demands much labor and care, but always ends in tranquillity and peace, because there is no agitation, no worry, when once the decision is made or the ruling accepted. For the resulting action is seen in the context of the total struggle between good and evil in the world, and therefore as part of the total divine strategy of love: you take always the long view; you live in the present and leave the future to God.

Those in authority must be meek

There is the same need of meekness when it is a question not of submitting to authority but of wielding authority. St. Augustine tells superiors that their desire should be to be loved rather than to be feared. Whatever the nature of the authority you have, you must use it not in order to treat other human beings as pawns, but in order to foster and cherish them as human hearts for which you are responsible to God. Every human relationship is an eternal responsibility. The greater the authority, the greater the number of laws by which it is answerable to God, and therefore the greater the need of obedience. The Pope is with accuracy called "the servant of the servants of God."

Every human being is unique: you cannot treat men and women as units in a neat scheme without doing violence to them. (Which is why there is something radically wrong with the sort of school in which each boy is precisely little more than a number: regimentation and education are incompatible.) If you are called upon to exercise authority over human beings, whether as parent or teacher or employer or ruler or pastor, the first thing to remember is that the essence of authority is responsibility to God for those you govern, and that you will be judged on love. The second thing is that if you regiment, you destroy because you ignore uniqueness.

Let us add a third thing, for there are some who think that authority necessarily means the harshness of an unbending and callous discipline. Our Lord said of Himself, "My yoke is sweet and my burden light" — and it is no business of ours to try to improve on Christ.[72]

Whether, then, you are commanding or obeying, you must be meek: the desire to dominate must be turned into the energy that *serves*. Yes, you have within you the instinct to leave the

[72] Matt. 11:30. There are times when you have to be severe, yes; but the saints know how to make even severity healing, consoling, and strengthening by making it the unambiguous expression of love; and even those of us who are far from holiness can save it from bitterness and destructiveness by keeping a sense of humor.

impress of your personality on your environment; but you can leave it, not in tyranny and violence, but in love and happiness. Instincts are in themselves neutral: it is the expression of them that is good or bad. Our business, therefore, is not to attempt to destroy them, but to attempt to build something of lasting value out of them.

Meekness gives strength

Meekness, like so many of these old Christian words, is often sadly misunderstood and therefore despised. Of course you will despise the thing if you think it means a lack of spirit and energy and strength. But it means the very opposite of these things. It means not false humility but the strength that can turn all energies to service of God and the world instead of the self; it means the strength of John the Baptist, defying kings and leading peoples, but knowing when the Christ comes that "He must increase, I must decrease."[73] It means using all the power and the gifts that God has given you, and not pretending that you have not, in fact, been given them; it means, therefore, having ambitions, zeal, and zest for great works.

But always behind the power and the ambition there is "Thy will be done."[74] The ambition is always to serve for love's sake; and the power is always primarily love-power, that inner power of the personality that you find in the saints, and that relies not on externals (such as riches or violence or a great

[73] John 3:30.

[74] Matt. 6:10.

parade), but on the abundance of the divinely given life within the spirit — the life that calls, but calls freely, to the heart. And that is the power that you can wield without fear, because it is a power which is *received*, and received only by the humble who can put on Christ.[75]

There is a danger that even the ambition to be a saint may be a self-willed and self-seeking ambition, but not if you have learned to be meek. For then you labor to the limits of your strength, you struggle to keep the Commandments and to grow in love and in prayer, but you are patient with yourself, you leave the results to God, and you do as well as you can at each successive moment. But whether or not you progress is a question you leave to Him.

Meekness includes poverty of spirit

Meekness, then, is poverty of spirit applied to the whole of life, to one's self, and even to the inner life of virtue. To care and not to care: the courage and strength of the love of the saints in spreading abroad in the world the spirit of love, and their meekness and humility in refusing to be upset by attacks upon them: these are the two aspects of a single unified life, the life of humility. To care and not to care: humility can love the whole world because it recognizes that the whole world is God's; and it is carefree because it has nothing to lose — not even its own self-respect.

Happy are the meek, for they shall possess the land. It is better, St. Thomas remarks, to possess than merely to inhabit.

[75] Gal. 3:27.

He sees the former as meaning "secure," unanxious possession, the sort of possession you know cannot be taken from you; and that is the sort of possession which is not something you *have* but something you *are*.

There must necessarily be moments when peace seems to be shattered and happiness seems infinitely remote; but learn to meet even the *lama sabachthanis*[76] of life as our Lord did — "not my will but Thine be done"[77] — and, in spite of misery at one level of the mind, you will preserve your peace and your joy in the deep places. You will be able to cast your cares upon Him, and to accept in humility whatever He wills to give or to take away, and so you will be able to go on serenely loving and serving the world, and making it happy.

[76] "Why hast Thou forsaken me?"; Matt. 27:46.

[77] Luke 22:42.

Family life and the gift of piety

Little children . . . a new commandment I give to you, that you love one another: as I have loved you, that you also love one another.[78]

Piety is another word which has fallen on evil days and lost its proper meaning. If you study its traditional theological sense, you will find nothing of that soft, sentimental escapism which the word seems to suggest nowadays. St. Thomas speaks of it as a part of justice: it is a question, therefore, of a plain, matter-of-fact duty — something you owe to something else; and that something else is clearly defined.

Justice itself is concerned with the exact payment of what you owe, but there are some debts that cannot, of their nature, be exactly repaid: you cannot repay God for all that He gives you, and so you speak of religion rather than of justice in His regard. You cannot repay the debt you owe your parents and fatherland, and so you speak not of justice so much as of *pietas*, of the virtue of piety. This is a question, first, of giving due honor, reverence, and devotion to your parents; but it includes

[78] John 13:33-34.

the matter-of-fact duty of seeing to their material welfare if they are in need, of caring for them when they are in ill health, and so on. Similarly, that part of piety which concerns one's fatherland is not a question of patriotic emotions but of real love and loving service.[79]

Piety lets us see God as our Father

What is the purpose of the *gift* of piety? St. Thomas tells us that as the virtue leads us to give due reverence and care to our parents, so the gift leads us to feel for God the love that a child feels for his father, according to the words of the Letter to the Romans, "You have received the spirit of adoption of sons, whereby we cry, 'Abba, Father.' "[80] The gift, then, gives us a relationship to God quite different from that implied in the virtue of religion: it is the sense of creatureliness, but with the addition now of the loving trust of the child for his father; it is awe, but with the addition of a sense of the closeness and

[79] The *patria* is still the land where we were born, the soil on which we depend and which is specially ours, the culture and traditions in which we share; it is still to our own country that we owe the greatest debt, and to which *pietas* properly refers. But as the world becomes, in some ways, more and more a unity, so the scope of *pietas* is enlarged: we owe, in degree, a debt to all the countries from which we benefit materially or culturally, and ultimately to the whole world. When we think of other nations in terms not of the political order but of the universality of the Church, present in all lands, then, of course, the national boundaries should sink further into insignificance. And while we cling to our own culture and traditions and feel a special duty to our own land, we cannot think of political progress except in terms of the good of the world as a whole.

[80] Rom. 8:15.

loving familiarity of the Infinite Father. Religion worships God the Creator and Lord from afar; here we are led — and led without pride or presumption because we are led precisely as a child — to that intimate relationship with God which the life of the Trinity makes possible: coheirs with Christ,[81] to share with and through Christ, therefore, in our own different way, in that same life of the Trinity.

It is this gift, then, in particular which brings about in us what we saw at the beginning as one of the essentials of the Christian life: the rebirth of the child. And it is this gift, also, which helps to bring about in us the corollary of that sonship: the love of the rest of God's family. The gift of piety, St. Thomas tells us, offers reverence and service not only to God, but also to men inasmuch as they belong to God. As a consequence, he adds, it leads us to help those who are in distress or misery.

The two things hang together. "If you love me, keep my commandments"; but the commandment on which all the others depend is the law of love not only of God but of our neighbor.[82] It is no good pretending to revere God as your Father unless you also in fact reverence and serve men as your brothers. The latter is, in practice, the criterion of the former.

We are called to make the world a happier place

Every human being is unique. It follows that every human being has some unique gift to give to his family: to his parents

81 Rom. 8:17.

82 John 14:15; Matt. 22:37-40.

and brothers and sisters in the ordinary narrow sense, first of all, and thence to his country and to the world. The small world of the human home is built up of the gifts of each member of it; the larger world without is built up, in the same way, of the various gifts — economic, political, cultural, and religious — of individual citizens.

If we are Christians, we must dismiss once and for all the idea that our business in the world is to serve ourselves and nobody else, to become holy ourselves and pay no attention to anyone else. Society is for man, yes; but there is a sense in which man is for society, too. We need society in order to grow to be fully men; but we need also to *serve* society in order to grow to be fully men. For without that life of service, we doom ourselves to selfishness; and in that way we shall never achieve wholeness.

When, therefore, we are considering what we shall do, whether in great things or in small, we cannot leave out of account the needs of the family. Sometimes it is our duty to give up what would indeed be very good for us if the pressing needs of home or of country demand our service instead.

Live your life in the unity of the home first of all. Train yourself to think in terms of what will make the home a better and a happier place. Then in your building up of the home, think of the needs and well-being of your immediate neighbors, and thence of your country and of the whole world. And so you will necessarily live a life of love, and fulfill that much at least — and it is a great deal — of the law of God.

Let us first think briefly of some of the ways in which we offend God by hurting, and perhaps destroying, the life of the family.

We must be charitable in speech

There is, first of all, anger, and the sins that spring from it: quarreling, contentions, and loud-voiced or contemptuous abuse. These things are easy to recognize and perhaps easy to regret.

But there are less obvious forms of the same vice which can do immense and perhaps irreparable harm to the family. There are people who are a burden to live with because, although they seldom fly into rages, they are touchy, choleric, swift to take offense in small ways over small things. There are those who, as St. Augustine remarks, are in a still less satisfactory state of soul because, although they are slow to take offense, they are slower also in asking pardon when ill temper has overcome them; they nurse their injuries and harbor grudges and brood over means of scoring a petty vengeance for a petty or perhaps an imaginary slight. This state of soul is a slow poison; and makes not only the life of the family impossible, but equally the life of worship of God. We are told that if we bring a gift to the altar and there remember that our brother has anything against us, we must leave the gift and go first to be reconciled, and only then return and offer it to God.[83]

We might meditate here on the use we make of wit and humor, for these, too, have to be judged in the light of the happiness of the family. Wit is a precious gift, and you must not let it lie fallow for fear of offending someone by it; but it demands a great delicacy of touch. There are occasions when the winds of wit have to be tempered to the shorn lambs.

[83] Matt. 5:23-24.

The same is true of humor, although it is less dangerous. It would be a tragedy to destroy it in you — what, indeed, is more valuable for a family life than humor? — but you have to be sure that love always shines through it, as it so easily can.

And when you come to the really cutting and mortifying uses of speech — to sarcasm and bitter irony and spite — then you are in a region where sin may easily be very grave. To have the power to spread laughter and gaiety about you is a lovely thing; its abuse is correspondingly hateful.

We must promote love and joy zealously

As with the tongue, so with the whole personality: it is a denial of *pietas* and a destruction of family life to be even in small ways difficult, prickly, unhelpful, aloof; it is a sign of great charity to be consistently the sunshine in the life of your family and in many other people's lives as well. Morality is thus, here as elsewhere, far from being a negative thing. Piety is not merely the avoidance of these sins of anger, but the positive duty of making others happy.

And we should not forget, either, that anger is only one of the opposing vices in this connection. There is also its opposite: a complete lack of zeal, an inability to be roused at all, a sort of stolid indifference to what goes on, whether good or ill. There is a proper time for anger, not in the sense of losing one's temper, but in the sense of a zeal to remedy abuses and to replace evil and hatred with love. This indeed is the proper use of the instinct which finds in the vice of anger its destructive expression: zeal attempts great and difficult things which demand high-spirited courage and even a sort of ruthlessness with oneself if they are to be done at all, for the sake of the family.

We must avoid envy and discord

There are the vices of envy and jealousy, which still more completely destroy the soul as well as the family. We should think, in this connection, of their minor forms — scandal-mongering, tale-bearing and spiteful gossip (how many characters have been taken away to the accompaniment of the tinkle of teacups?) — which lead to the greater sins, and eventually perhaps to real hatred.

We should beware here of unconscious motivations: it is so easy to persuade ourselves that what we say *has* to be said for the good of the persons concerned, whereas in reality we are only scoring over them or humiliating them. And what is the true use of the instinct here? You find it in St. Thomas's courteously benign explanation of St. Jerome's[84] advice to Laeta about her daughter's education: "Let her have companions that she may learn with them, envy them and be nettled when they are praised." "Envy here," St. Thomas says, "means that zeal with which we ought to strive to progress with those who are better than we."[85] There is such a thing as holy emulation, although no doubt it is not an easy thing to acquire.

There is the still worse sin of discord: still worse because if it is bad to hurt one of your brothers by destroying love between him and yourself, it is yet more diabolical — more

[84] Biblical scholar and Doctor of the Church (c. 342-420).

[85] *Summa Theologica*, II-II, Q. 36, art. 2.

characteristic of the Devil — to hurt two or more of your brothers and destroy the love they have for one another. "Six things there are which the Lord hateth . . . and the seventh His soul detesteth, namely, him that soweth discord among brethren."[86]

Piety calls us to avoid extremes in our manners

There are still other ways in which we can fail in piety toward our family. It is important to remind ourselves that deliberate bad manners can be a sin against charity: an indulgence in that sort of vulgarity which, because it is strident, grates upon people's nerves and can cause real distress, or in the type of mannerism which, so far from being a charming or amusing idiosyncrasy, is a trial to those we live with.

Consider the priggishness which is a form of pride, and the snobbishness which, because it judges people at best on unessentials, is a form of blindness. There is the sin of ingratitude, and taking other people's devotion or self-sacrifice for granted as our due.

There is the sort of isolation which is reserve gone mad: you may be kindly enough disposed inside yourself, but your manner is such that people hesitate a long time before appealing to you for help, because you give the impression that you do not want to be disturbed and put out. This is akin to the vice of "incuriosity" of which St. Thomas treats, which implies a sort of mental stagnation as far as social life is concerned, a lack of zest and interest which is also a lack of charity and

[86] Prov. 6:16, 19.

responsibility, and denotes a lost childhood — the soul grown old and stale. You cannot be living in love and piety if nothing outside yourself has interest for you.

On the other hand there is the vice of curiosity, which is the wrong sort of desire for information. It may be wrong because it is proud: you want to know all about people and things because it feeds your sense of power. It may be wrong because it is dissipated, distracting you from more important things, or because it is a form of trespassing — that ruthless inquisitiveness to which nothing is sacred (people sometimes need to be reminded that to read letters not addressed to them may well be a grave sin). It may be wrong because it is directed to scandalmongering and gossip. It is wrong if in any way it is the expression not of a loving interest in others' lives but of an antisocial inability to mind one's own business.

You must preserve or recapture the childlike quality of concern for the family, but always distinguish it from the insatiable flutter-pated inquisitiveness which can never bear to be unacquainted with whatever is going on, however unimportant or however private.

To end this examination of conscience, let us consider some of the remaining ways in which, by excess or defect, you can fail to be the sort of person who makes family life what it ought to be, a continual joy.

You will fail if you are glum, and never have a word of encouragement or gratitude or praise, or even a word at all, for those around you. On the other hand, you will fail if you are garrulous and boring, producing a constant stream of meaningless small talk which swirls about the heads of your relatives until they feel submerged and stifled.

There is a point at which untidiness becomes a sin, because it causes real discomfort and inconvenience to others. There is, on the other hand, the finicky tidiness, the passion for quite unnecessary exactitude, which can never bear to see anything a millimeter out of its proper position, and must have every household event timed to the second, and the home itself bound tightly in domestic red tape.

You are impious if you are cold and unresponsive, but also if you gush. It is a sin to be testy, but there can be also a dangerous lack of solicitude in that sort of thoughtless and bovine heartiness which administers heavy slaps on the back at the breakfast table, or in the loud jocularity which is insensible to the needs of a quieter mood. Moreover, while it is a horrible thing to be thin-lipped and humorless, it is at least a very dangerous thing to be a practical joker — and almost certain to be boring. These things, if they are hardly to be classed as sins, at least could be regarded as imperfections.

Similarly, people who are darkly secretive are a pest, and people who tend to be shocked are worse. But indiscretion and a complete lack of reticence are not lovely qualities either.

Finally, there are people who have to dominate the household and control whatever is going on, and always take the center of the stage. And there are others who have no spirit and contribute nothing to the common life. Both types are lacking in piety.

It is important to remind ourselves often that the cultivation of a right sense of humor can be one of the forms of piety. Cultivate a sense of humor in yourself about other people, and in other people about yourself: learn to laugh rather than be vexed by other people's foibles, but learn the ability also to let other people laugh at your own. It is not a virtue to be uncritical, but you have to be sure that your judgments are not hasty or spiteful, and that the growth of the power of criticism is accompanied by a growth in gentleness. By learning to be pious and to love, you will acquire the sort of personality that people will instinctively take their troubles to.

Piety gives us a sense of God's Providence

This piety toward the family and thence toward the greater world outside is a virtue; but we need the gift as well if we are to practice it fully and spontaneously. If you learn to treat God as your Father, you will automatically come to think of men as your brothers, and to love them as your brothers precisely in the unity of God's family, so that your love for them and for Him is one single love.

Piety toward God gives us a constant and inclusive sense of the *Providence* of God: we learn to see every event as His will, and to accept it as such. It is not, of course, that we have no ambitions, and make no effort to achieve what seems to us to be good, but whether our efforts meet with success or with failure, and however things we have no control over turn out, we see in them all the guiding hand of God. We accept them with carefree trust and confidence, since all that we have and are, and all that we want and love and cherish, is secure in the eternal present of His mercy.

This is indeed the very essence of the life of religion as opposed to the life of self-will: the growth toward that complete identity of will, that complete abandonment of self to the saving and sustaining arms of God, of which the mystics tell us. Without it, we can never learn to care and not to care, and never live in that peace which the world cannot give.

There is no such thing as chance; we tend to think too readily in terms of accident and coincidence and fate and "the way things turn out," and so perhaps we miss many an indication of the way our duty lies, and many an opportunity to do service to love.

This sense of the pervasive Providence of God is a thing we have to learn by constant reference and attention: whatever happens is His will, and has a meaning, and is meant to be of use. Whatever happens will be turned eventually to good in His restoring and redemptive power. Whatever happens, therefore, I must accept with equanimity in my deepest heart, however sad or tragic it may be, because in Him all things are one, and there is nothing that escapes His Providence and lies outside His purposes for the world. Our Father . . . Thy will be done: the two things go together; it is because we say the first that we can hope to mean the second.

All this can come only after a long and arduous effort to be faithful to God's help in all the small events of life. It depends on growth in prayer and courage and patience. But if we can gradually school ourselves to take everything thus with docility and peace from God, we shall at the same time learn to be equable and at peace with men. Piety toward God implies and causes piety toward men. Again, it is not that we must have no ambitions of our own or make no effort to influence situations and events — far from it. But when, in fact, our efforts are unrewarded, when people are difficult or antagonistic and cause us sorrow, we shall not be flustered, desperate, or hopelessly depressed, because we shall know that this, too, is in

God's hands, and that we must not worry. And we shall go on thinking of mankind as our family.

We must be pious in prayer

The life of action is dependent on the life of prayer. To have the quality of piety in our lives, we must have the quality of piety in our prayer. We must take the prayer of awe a step farther. God remains the *mysterium tremendum* before whom we are as nothing, but He is also our Father. The awed fear of the child in face of the unknown becomes the reverential love of a known person, a Father. "Hallowed be Thy name":[87] the Transcendent is near to us because we can name Him; and very near to us because the name is Father, and calls forth from us confidence and trust and love. But it is still the confidence and trust and love of the child.

Piety enables us to see the world as our family

Piety, then, is a necessary quality of our attitude both to God and to men. And in the last resort the two things become one: for we best acknowledge the fatherhood of God when we acknowledge it in the company of our brothers. We pray best, and we labor best, when we pray and labor as a family. "Wherever two or three are gathered together in my name . . ."[88]

We should stop sometimes and think (at Mass especially), "I am praying with my family," for it will color our attitude

[87] Matt. 6:9; Luke 11:2.

[88] Matt. 18:20.

toward our family. We should think of it also because zeal is infectious. If we pray fervently ourselves, we may help others, and equally, if we pray fervently, it may be because we are *being helped* by others. For the same reasons, we should cherish particularly the old tradition of family prayers, for these can sanctify the home as nothing else can; they can make the home a real unity in love and make family life a real worship of God.

At the end, we shall be judged on love. Love of the family, small and great, is the test of our love of God. Our Lord said of Mary the sinner that much was forgiven her because she had loved much.[89] It is a lovely epitaph to be called a great lover of God and of men. And if, through our lives, we have labored hard to love and serve those with whom our life has brought us into contact, then He will surely say of us at the end that much is forgiven us, too, because we have loved Him and shown our love by loving His family.

[89] Luke 7:47.

C. The Sacrament of this Beatitude

Confirmation

But the Paraclete, the Holy Spirit, whom the Father will send in my name, He shall teach you all things, and suggest unto you all things whatsoever I shall say to you. . . . Let not your heart be troubled, nor fear.[90]

If we are thinking of our duties toward our family and God's, it is natural that we should think of the sacrament of Confirmation, since it is precisely the sacrament of the social life of the Christian, the sacrament which fits him to be a full member of the family.

Let us look first of all at the symbolism. We are meant to see the sacrament as a repetition of the first Whitsuntide:[91] the Paraclete, the Strengthener, comes not indeed, as it were, in tongues of fire nor to give us the gift of tongues, but with similar energizing and encouraging purpose, to "kindle within us the fire of His love," that we, being re-created, may be used by Him to renew the face of the earth.[92]

[90] John 14:26, 27.

[91] The week beginning with Whitsunday, or Pentecost, the feast of the Descent of the Holy Spirit upon the Apostles (Acts 2:1-4).

[92] Ps. 103:30 (RSV = Ps. 104:30).

Confirmation gives us strength and spiritual maturity

It is the sacrament of social action; but social action begins when responsibility begins: when we grow up. It is the sacrament of adolescence. That is when you begin to gain your freedom and independence; when, in consequence, you have to face the greater world and decide whether to allow it to mold you or whether you are strong enough to impress your personality upon it as a responsible man, an artist and creator of new life.

The results of this first encounter with a perhaps hostile, perhaps pernicious environment can be so far-reaching, and it is so easy to fail and to be submerged, that you need all the help you can get: you need the strength and the fire of the Spirit to retain your integrity and increase your abundance of life.

Confirmation is meant to help us here. But it has also its purely supernatural purpose: it is meant not only to help us meet the particular problems of adolescence but also to make us spiritually mature. The grace is given as *power*, and all the symbolism is military symbolism: the anointing with oil for the warrior spirit, the signing on the forehead to drive out fear, the tap on the cheek for the virile bearing of hardships, and the idea of fire — heat — following on the baptismal water, to signify growth.

Confirmation calls us to help others become holy

What is the purpose of this growth and fire and strength? The reference is always to the family, to the world in need of restoration. The power is not merely given for our own private sanctification; it is given in order that we may be able to help others to become holy by becoming holy ourselves. You have to *fight* as a soldier — although to fight, let us remember at once, with the weapons of love — and to fight as a soldier means necessarily to fight for somebody else, to fight for a cause.

That is what these qualities are for; that is what the maturity of soul and of conscience is for. You cannot fight as you ought in the age-long struggle between good and evil unless you know what the struggle is about; unless you have initiative and can bear responsibility; and unless you are strong enough to accept dangers and hardships lightheartedly and not be dismayed.

Confirmation leads to social action

Confirmation is the sacrament of social action. You are meant, through the power it confers, to be able henceforth to contribute actively and creatively to the family life of the Church and of the world.

You must be meek and pious; but that does not mean being a blind fool waiting for an order before you can move, or being lost and panic-stricken as soon as you are left to yourself. You must be obedient to the authority of the Church, but it is the obedience of the free man that is demanded of you. You cannot expect a direct inspiration from God or a direct lead from His representatives on earth in every little event and circumstance of life: it is part of your duty, as a mature Christian, to be able to apply the things you believe about God to the things you have to do among men.

Confirmation is the sacrament of the common priesthood of the laity: every Christian is meant to share in degree in the priesthood of Christ, as we shall see in detail later on. Every Christian is called to be with Christ as mediator, to help in the redemptive work of Christ in the world, and to lead the world back to love through love.

And that means that he must have knowledge, bravery, initiative, and persevering strength; but they must be gifts received and must be fruits of docility to the Spirit. It is the meek who, possessing the land, can sanctify and sweeten the land. It is those who obey the Spirit through the gift of piety who can give a full and creative service to the family. It is those who have filled their hearts with the sense of God's continuous care and Providence — and so have identified their wills with His, and can live with a carefree abandon to His good pleasure — who can do in the world the will of the Father in union with the Son.

When you think of the Christian duty of social action, when you think of the apostolate of the laity, think first of the upper room in which the timorous apostles were huddled in hiding. It was to these immature souls that the Spirit came, and through them that the Spirit worked to such effect that their "sound went forth into the whole world, and their words to the ends of the world."[93] You must fight for the cause of love with the weapons of love, and for the cause of poverty of spirit and meekness with poor and humble means. There is something a little suspicious about schemes of social action which begin with a grandiose display and a grandiose expenditure,

[93] Ps. 18:5 (RSV = Ps. 19:4).

with heavily embossed notepaper and offices at a smart London address. There may, indeed, be nothing wrong with that; but at least make sure that behind it all there is what matters most and what alone will do work for God: the selfless zeal and the consuming fire of God-filled men and women.

Social action depends more on our being than on our doing

There is always the danger that we may think we can do the work of the Spirit in the world by purely external activity, by being busy about many things,[94] without bothering at all about what we are and what we love. That is why we have thought in such detail of the ways in which we can fail our family, fail in piety. If this is not as it should be, our work for the world will certainly not be what it should be. People are not deceived by an imposing façade for long: they look for the living substance behind the appearances, and the more ambitious the appearances, the more they will rightly expect to find behind them. If we challenge them thus to look and allow them to be disappointed, we are doing not the Spirit's work but the Devil's.

Being is more important than doing. You can be an apostle and use to the full the grace of Confirmation, even if you belong to no society and no social organization within the Church: you can be an apostle by *being* the sort of person whose loving absorption in the presence of God and loving obedience to the will of God is apparent to all who have eyes

[94] Luke 10:41.

to see. And on the other hand, you will never be an apostle and never be faithful to the sacrament, unless you are that, even if you join with zest in every form of Catholic Action[95] you can find.

Let us be simple about all this, and go back to the simplest things for our pattern. Who really shows *pietas* towards his family, his neighbors, and his friends? It is not necessarily the man who does a great deal: he may be a nuisance; he may intrude and may poison his service with condescension.

Piety must be, first of all, a quality of being: being the sort of person who is felt to be loving, interested, sympathetic, and anxious to help when help is required. And the actual carrying out of that will to serve — precisely because it is always the expression of a state of being (and can never be simply a parade) — is necessarily a form of piety because it is a form of reverence and love.

Our holiness helps others to become holier

The purpose of Confirmation is to enable us to help others to be holy by *being* holy ourselves. The primary purpose of Catholic Action is to carry forth into the world the power of a God-filled personality — *organum pulsatum a Spiritu sancto*. If you want to be used by the Spirit in His work in the world, there is one essential preliminary: you must be meek; you must have docility.

The apostolate of reason is always a necessity: there is always need of those who can explain and defend the Faith,

[95] Organized religious activity on the part of the laity.

and state it in terms which can be understood by the contemporary mind. Indeed it may be that this necessity weighs upon us now more than ever before. And yet perhaps it is not the supreme task of today. The world gets very tired of argument. It would be more accurate to say that the labors of reason *alone* are not the supreme task, and that the world gets very tired of argument which springs only from the head. You need to have a very firm, clear grasp of the truth and to be able to state it clearly; but if you want people not only to listen politely but to keep your words in their hearts and be changed by them, then you must become, through the power of the Spirit, the sort of person who draws people and disturbs and uproots them without their knowing why, because you are what you are.

The supreme task of today is a question of being, because it is a question of bringing back to the world the direct *experience* of the power of love in the world — of bringing it face to face with the immensity of the Paraclete, the Strengthener, filling and shining through the bodies of men. When you have been shaken to the roots of your being by the mere presence of someone who stands for a truth, you are impelled to examine the truth he stands for and are predisposed to apprehend it. "Kindle within them the *fire* of Thy love"; then "they shall be re-created, and Thou shalt renew the face of the earth."

Unity and charity in the family lead to unity and charity in the world

The Holy Spirit comes down at Pentecost upon the Christian family, bringing a common power and fire for the common task. That is the best way we can work as Christians in the world: to be first a family, and then, as a family unity, to serve the larger family of the world. There is no short cut. You bring your own unique contribution to your home and help to build up its unity and its charity. Then your home, in its turn, helps to build the unity and charity of your country, so that your country, too, if it is faithful to its vocation, may bring its contribution to the life, and help to forge the unity, of the world.

That is your task in the kingdom of this world. And in and through that work, you have your work for the Church, and it follows the same lines. Through your family life, family worship, and family prayer, you help to build up the life of your parish and of the whole Catholic community in your country, and so eventually of the Church as a whole. And whether you think of this creative work in terms of the home, the parish, the country, or the Church, it is always the same thing in the end: love flinging wide the doors to those outside, quietly anxious to heal and help, quietly ready to fulfill the will of God in this life of service, humbly grateful for being allowed to serve.

We must radiate the Church's joy and fellowship

Just because *love* and *hatred* are abstract nouns, we must not minimize their power. The world is filled with the spirit of evil, with hatred; and it is a real influence in the world, which can be felt as a bleak wind is felt, even though we may not be actually conscious of its effect upon us. But there is love in the world, too, although so little of it in men compared with the world's need: and that, too, has its often unconscious effect on the souls of men. That is what we must increase and intensify as a part, and perhaps the chief part, of our apostolate, and the work of our common priesthood, so that when the Faith is mentioned, it may suggest more to the non-Christian than a system of beliefs, a view of reality: it may recall, primarily, the power which is love-power, the feeling that in the company of Christ's followers, there is life, joy, and welcome; that the Church is not an alien and forbidding territory upon which it is unpleasant to trespass, but, on the contrary, a place which seems immediately familiar and tranquilizing, and a place of peace, because as soon as you enter it, and without having to look much about you, you realize what you had not realized fully before — that the Church is home.

Chapter Five

Blessed are they who mourn, for they shall be comforted.

Matt. 5:5

Mourning with others

We have been considering our Lord's reply to those who think of happiness in terms either of possessions or of the proud fulfillment of the aggressive instinct; St. Thomas, when he deals with this third beatitude, explains it in terms of the way in which creatures can be the occasion of our turning from God, if we regard them as the highest good, and in particular of the search for pleasure, the delight and appeasement of the senses.

Our own comfort and well-being must not be our highest priority

We might perhaps think here of one particular — and perhaps particularly dangerous because insidious — way in which the demands of the senses can exercise a sort of tyranny over us: the search for comfort, not so much in the sense of material self-indulgence, as in the sense of a determination to arrange one's own life pleasantly, to feather one's nest, and then to let nothing and nobody interfere with its quiet and harmonious course. For this can indeed turn a man from God, and become itself his highest good, to which everything else must be sacrificed.

You can be kindly, for example, and even positively kind, so as perhaps to deceive even the elect, but your kindness stops dead at the point at which your nicely planned mode of life is interfered with. You can be friendly, and even have a great gift for making friends, but sooner or later it becomes clear that instead of loving your friends, you use them. You can be sympathetic, benevolent, patriotic, and religious-minded, but always with this reservation: you keep these things in their place, and their place is the carefully allotted place your egotistic scheme of things allows them. You will not have your comfort invaded at any price. If that is the case, you are not in the company of those who mourn; on the contrary, you are still in the service of mammon.

The Christian must die in order to be reborn, and the death is the death of the self that sets itself up to be independent — to be a god, and to use all things as its creatures, for profit or pleasure. Here we think, in particular, of the search for pleasure: you will use things, and be quite prepared incidentally to be fond of them, just so long as they fit in with your scheme and minister to your comfort. But that is not the Christian attitude. It is on love that the "whole law depends";[96] and this condescending affection which uses things on condition is not love.

In love every getting is a form of giving; this other attitude is a sort of lust, where every giving is only a form of, or a means to, getting. The center is yourself. In love the center is always

[96] Matt. 22:40.

the other, and you are identified only with the other. The pleasure-seeker in this sense is enslaved to the original sin: he has yet to die, to make the long journey and slay the serpent, and find himself anew and truly in the Other. There is no love without reverence; but reverence consists in saying, "It is *you* who are important."

Mourning with others calls for reverence toward creatures

Blessed are the meek: you have not left this beatitude behind when you come to the next one; you will not be of the company of those who mourn unless you have learned to be humble. And humility in this context is a humility about and toward the things that surround you. You must reverence reality, and so in your use or enjoyment of it, you must be temperate.

Temperateness, as we shall see, is not the quenching or diluting of passion, but the deepening of it. Temperateness is not allowing passion to dissipate itself in meandering shallows, or to become isolated from the full personal life, but, on the contrary, it means making passion essentially a part of the wholeness of the body-spirit, and essentially, therefore, a part of the body-spirit's worship of God. Passion cannot be worship of God unless it is reverence toward its immediate earthly object. And just as piety toward creatures is the test of piety toward God, so with reverence. If you want to be among those who mourn, you must start by making sure that you are temperate in your attitude toward creatures, that you are reverent toward men and women, animals, and inanimate things.

You must not be sentimental: you must not make reverence synonymous with fear or softness or blindness. There is an order in created things, and the less are meant to serve the greater, and to serve them according to their nature. It is not reverence but irreverence to treat your pets as though they were beings of a superior order: it is a failure to respect their nature. It is not reverence but irreverence to refuse from mistaken humanitarianism to punish a disobedient child. But you can be reverent to the nature and personality of the child you are punishing, although it is a very different reverence from the reverence the child owes to you.

We must subordinate our desires to the needs of others

Blessed are the meek, then, because in this question of our attitude toward things, the meek have the power to be humble, and therefore to be temperate. But this present beatitude takes us further than that. The gift, St. Thomas points out, goes further than the virtue and enables us to cast off desire altogether, if need be, or even to choose discomfort and sorrow. You are so far from subordinating everything to your own comfort and well-being that, on the contrary, you subordinate these readily and gladly to the needs of others. You are so far from refusing to have your life invaded that you yourself are always leaving it to give help to others. You are so far from determining to "keep yourself to yourself," you are so far from regarding your own private life as a sacred preserve, that, on the contrary, you have learned the essential Christian lesson that all that you do and all that you are affects the rest of the world, and the rest of the world is your family. You are your brother's keeper.[97]

Those who mourn are comforted even in this life

Let us note at once: they shall be comforted. The quest of invulnerability, the search for a comfortable life beyond interference, the refusal to be put out by anything or anybody: these will bring not comfort but misery, because their end is isolation and death of soul. Oh yes, you will be undisturbed if this is your object; and unless you are so dead as to have no feeling left, you will cry out for someone, however uncomfortable, to share your loneliness and your misery with you. But they who mourn shall be comforted; and they shall be comforted, not simply by a subsequent reward, a belated consolation prize for what they have suffered, but because their sorrow itself will be *turned into* joy[98] even on earth, the sort of joy that gives life, strength, courage, and exhilaration.

They shall be strengthened. Once again modern use has debased the language: we think of comfort first of all in terms

[97] Cf. Gen. 4:9. There are, of course, degrees of responsibility. A man is responsible in strict justice for his children, for example; he cannot have the same obligation toward strangers to whom he is in no way related. The demands of charity, too, have their degrees of urgency. But the lesson of the gospel is that there is no human need, and no human evil, which can leave us entirely unmoved. Our love of God and our divine sonship make us a family. We each have a share in the responsibilities of the family as a whole; charity must make us feel the need of helping in suffering wherever we meet it, sharing in the penalties of sin wherever we come across them, and joining at least by our prayer in the general burden of sin and sorrow in the world.

[98] Jer. 31:13; John 16:20.

of material things — an easy chair, cushions, soft slippers. And then, when we speak of somebody giving comfort, we think of a soothing influence, a smoothing away of cares, which has something similarly soft about it. These things have their place, the second one especially, in the idea of being comforted, but they are secondary.

Comfort includes strengthening

The Paraclete, the Comforter, is not primarily a soothing influence. The word itself means a strengthening: it is, if you will, a soothing influence — this is sometimes a necessity — but only *in order* to give renewed courage and strength to face the reality which has overwhelmed the sufferer.

And here perhaps is a clue to our Lord's apparent paradox. Blessed are they who are ready and anxious to go to great lengths and endure great discomfort in order to bring strength and courage to others: for in giving these things to others, they will themselves receive them. To encourage another to great deeds is to be strengthened yourself. And (lest we lose sight of the gentler side of comfort in stressing the stronger) there are few things that bring greater balm and peace to the soul than to bring them to the soul of another — as the confessor knows so well by experience.

We must recognize our solidarity in guilt

But how are we to bring ourselves to obey the Spirit's promptings so as to be able to comfort, and, in general, to suffer with not only the few who are dear to us, but the many who are in need? We must go back to the thought of our solidarity in sin and our duty to share in the redemptive work of Christ. We share in the guilt of the world; we must share in the suffering for which the guilt is responsible.

It is not for us to try to assess our precise measure of guilt; no one can tell that but God. We may not be among the spectacular sinners, but we do not know whether their sins are less heavy on their souls than our smaller sins are on our souls, for we do not know whether grace has abounded in us immensely more than in them. It is easy to say, "He has murdered and I have not; so he is a greater criminal than I"; but no one can say, "He has murdered and I have not, and therefore he is a greater *sinner* than I."

We come back, then, to the sense of sin; for if we really understood the sin that is in us, we would not be in any mood to attempt to assess our particular degree of responsibility for the guilt and pain of the world. That is why the sense of personal sin and personal responsibility grows greater as you come nearer to holiness; and that is why the idea of measuring guilt against guilt is in the last resort irrelevant. What Christ did we must try to do: and He, being guiltless, took upon Himself all guilt. We are each, in Him, responsible for all.

We are called to share in redemptive suffering

But to be responsible is more than to share in guilt and consequent suffering: it is to share in *redemptive* suffering, the sort of suffering that helps to *take away* the sin of the world. Go back to the simple facts of ordinary human sympathy: love is unhappy if it is *not* sharing in the other's pain. But why? It is not simply because, through the identity of heart and will, when one suffers, the other automatically suffers too, but also because the sharing is felt to be a helping, a strengthening, and a comforting.

And if you are living in God, and therefore see His family as your family also, you will be impelled to feel thus about all His children: nothing human will be alien to you, and in particular no human cross will be a matter of indifference to you. You will want to share the sufferings of all because you will share God's love for all.

Blessed are they who mourn: but to do that in the gospel sense, you must become the sort of person to whom others spontaneously take their troubles; and there is only one way to do that. You will find others anxious to share their troubles with you if you desire to share them; and you will desire to share them if you love.

The Commandments call us to positive action

Blessed are they who mourn. We should see the Commandments in this light; for while in themselves they state the negative minimum, charity carries them right over to the positive maximum: not only that you must not be intemperate and selfish in your desires, but that you must be ready, if need be, to set aside your desires altogether, and even to choose discomfort and sorrow. It is not enough that you should not do murder: you must be ready to lay down your own life for your brethren. It is not enough that you should not steal: you must be ready to give of your own possessions when your brethren are in need. It is not enough that you should not commit adultery: you must be ready even to give up your own family life and its comforts if God calls you in that way to serve your brethren. It is not enough that you should refrain from covetousness: you must have the positive quality of poverty of spirit. It is not enough that you should not take away your neighbor's name and character: you must be ready, if need be, to become yourself an outcast if love demands it of you.

All that divine recklessness which you find in the saints is in this beatitude: being poor in spirit, they are not tied down by possessions; being meek, they are not held back by self-respect; but being of those who mourn, they are yet more fully free, because they want to hold back nothing for themselves — of time or trouble, of ease or security — and so they can give all they have and all they are to their brethren.

And they are comforted: they are strengthened and consoled, not when their troubles are over, but *in* their troubles, because, in the first place, their labors are the labors of love, which is its own reward, and because, in the second place, their sorrows have an instant response of love and gratitude from those they have helped — including God Himself.

Sharing in atonement for sins enlarges our hearts

There is a third reason. As there is a solidarity in sin, so there is a solidarity in atonement. Those who mourn are helping to bring souls to God through their love, through helping them to bear their crosses as Simon of Cyrene helped our Lord.[99]

[99] Matt. 27:32; Mark 15:21; Luke 23:26.

But to take up a cross for and with another is to turn it into a tree of life. There are things you will never know, never understand, except through suffering, and especially through suffering with another. Knowledge is not perfect until it becomes love-knowledge; and the way to the deepest love-knowledge is through suffering. You cannot know the depths of reality until you have been down to the depths of reality; but you learn most when it is with and for another that you go.

This need not be a conscious sharing between two particular human beings, although this is the easiest way. There is a solidarity in atonement. The most practical application of all that we have been thinking is indeed this: that whatever suffering and sorrow may come to you, and whenever it may come, it can be used, and ought to be used, in the power and company of Christ for the healing and comforting of the world as a whole; and in that sharing of the sorrow of the world as a whole, you can find your understanding and your heart immeasurably enlarged, enlarged indeed to something remotely approaching the fullness of the stature of Christ.

They shall be comforted. "It is more to be comforted in the kingdom than merely to have and possess it," says St. Thomas; "for there are many things the possession of which is accompanied with sorrow."[100] One of them is love. But the sorrow that love brings in its train can so easily be this strengthening and upbuilding sorrow, the sorrow that heals and renews; and that sort of sorrow is comforted because it is itself a thing of joy.

To lust after more and more things for the sake of the pleasure they can give; to cling more and more to things or to

[100] *Summa Theologica*, I-II, Q. 69, art. 4.

a settled and pleasurable way of life because of the material comfort that is in them: this is to have more and more care, and more and more loneliness, and therefore more and more sorrow. But to share more and more deeply in the all-inclusive love and sympathy and suffering of God is indeed to have sorrows, but to have sorrows that are turned immediately and inevitably into joy because they are the stuff of vision and understanding and love, and in the glory of the vision and the love, they glow with fire.

Single-mindedness and the gift of knowledge

For in his hand are both we, and our words, and all wisdom, and the knowledge and skill of works. For he hath given me the true knowledge of the things that are: to know the disposition of the whole world, and the virtues of the elements, the beginning and ending, and the midst of the times.[101]

They who mourn, who can forget their own desires altogether if need be, or even choose discomfort and sorrow, in order to serve Love in all things, are the ones who in actual practice achieve wisdom. This is because they have brought the manifold into unity by seeing God in all things and by turning their love and service of all things into a single act of worship of the One.

St. Thomas associates this beatitude with the gift of knowledge, because, he says, the gift leads us to mourn over the way we have allowed creatures to distract us from God: we have turned them into a means of comfort or pleasure, and so enjoyed them apart from and in opposition to God.

"He sees God aright who sees Him in all things." The gift of knowledge enables us to judge of everyday things and events from God's point of view. Seeing Him in all things, and seeing

[101] Wisd. 7:16-18.

them, therefore, in the light of the eternal present as His handiwork and His habitation, we judge of them not as though they were our creatures to be used as we please, but as part of our worship of Him. But to do that is at once to dethrone the pleasure principle and to accept a standard of judgment, and acquire an attitude of mind, in direct contradiction to it. We are only stewards.

Let us recall, first of all, what sort of a judgment this is. The gifts are given to us to correct and supplement our natural powers. There are two ways in which virtues are imperfect in us. First, we possess them imperfectly, and this imperfection is removed by greater fervor of life, and therefore a more complete possession of the virtuous habits.

Secondly, there is an inescapable imperfection in the habits themselves: they are God-given, but they have to bow to the limitations of human faculties and the human reason. And so faith, for example, is in itself obscure, and prudence and temperateness are limited by the ability of the mind to decide what the prudent or the temperate course of action is in any given case. This second imperfection can be removed only by the presence of a higher habit in the soul: the presence, in fact, of the direct impulse and guidance of the Spirit.

When we speak, then, of the gift of knowledge, we leave far behind us the mental ability which comes of book-learning or the analysis of experience by a keen intellect: we are in the realm of the wisdom which comes directly from God, and which you are likely to find in the unlettered and simple more often perhaps than in the brilliant and the learned, since it is the fruit of the soul's docility to God. When you find a poor peasant woman, unable to read or write or understand abstruse matters, but who startles you by the deep penetration and the sureness of touch with which she judges human affairs, motives, and duties in the light of divine truth, then you can feel you are watching the workings of the gift of knowledge. It is not a rational judgment so much as a sort of intuition, which comes of living with God and so learning, unconsciously, to share His mind.

There are four ways in which this gift can help us to be single-minded, to see all the manifold in terms of the One, and to avoid being distracted.

Knowledge helps us to see God correctly

First of all, it can help us in our judgments about God Himself. We are dependent, at the beginning, for our knowledge of God on the formulas of the Faith; and these formulas are created things, necessarily inadequate expressions of the Infinite Reality. It is not these we believe in, but the things they strive to express; nonetheless if we misunderstand them, if we read the wrong implications into them, we shall be misled about the Reality. There is always the danger of projecting onto God the purely human qualities, emotions, motivations, and standards with which we are familiar. There are always the dangers of sentimentality, self-deception, and wishful thinking.

The gift of knowledge can help us to keep a sense of God in all our derivative judgments about Him; it can call us back to the central core of truth if our speculations go awry; it can keep alive and active in us the immediate apprehension of God, which guides and determines all our thought about God.

Knowledge helps us to see creatures correctly

Then, in the second place, the gift of knowledge causes us to judge aright about creatures in themselves, neither despising them (which might mean affronting God their Maker) nor idolizing them (which would mean turning our backs on Him). They are not just means to our own pleasure or profit; nor are they our final end. This is easy enough to grasp in theory, but very difficult to live up to in practice. We badly need the constant guidance of the Spirit. How are we in practice to love creatures, and especially men and women, as we ought, and yet not make them a distraction from God? How are we to bring *this* manifold to unity?

We have already seen the answer in the first chapter, where the doctrine of Christian detachment was discussed: the love from which, with much grace and much labor, the evil of self-love can little by little be expelled, so that in the end it may become wholly a part of the love of God. Here we need only notice the special danger of the kind of love in which the senses and feelings are involved, because of the special difficulty of supernaturalizing these and restraining their tendency to lead us into independence and defiance of God. If they are part of a true personal love, and if they are adequately governed and guided by the spirit, they can give to love a great power to influence for good, to lead to God. This is their proper function; and only thus can they be purified and supernaturalized.

Consequently, we have to avoid the danger of sentimentality, which means that emotion is isolated and made an end in itself, so that there is no sharing in thought and will. Emotion, therefore, ceases to be functional; it ceases to play its part in helping the shared life of thought and will to come nearer to God. The relationship is sterile, and instead of becoming gradually a part of the love of God, it will, in fact, become inevitably more and more sickly until it dies away altogether.

Still more, we have to avoid the danger of sensuality, which means that sense-pleasure is isolated and made an end in itself, so that not only is indulgence sought apart from God, but in the relationship itself, there is no sharing of thought or will or even feeling. There is not only no growth in the unity of mind and heart which leads to God; there is no unity at all, but only isolated individual indulgence. It is not only not love of God; it is love of nothing but oneself.

But when these dangers are fought against and the emotions and senses are trained to fulfill their proper function, then the love which includes them, so far from being a distraction from God, can be a powerful incentive to know and love Him better. And it is all the more powerful precisely because of its wholeness: you are engaged, not just with one element of your nature, but with your whole personality.

It remains only too true that all this is difficult to achieve consistently in practice. You need the help of the Spirit, because not only the senses and emotions but the self as a whole want, at times, to be autonomous, to forget about poverty of spirit and meekness and discomfort. And you may well need the help of the Spirit, too, to save you from making these immediate preoccupations exclusive of the world outside. You will ensure that they are finally right and Godward-turning if you ensure that they lead you not to love others less and be less ready to let them invade your life, but to love them more. And you will be doing the best thing you can to ensure that, in all your love, you love not only well but wisely if you remember the gift of knowledge, which is given to the docile soul, so that, living always in the presence of God, you learn to listen always to His voice.

Knowledge directs our path to holiness

The third thing with which the gift of knowledge can help us is the whole matter of the *technique* of our journey to God. We act as we ought when our actions are really an expression of the realities in which we believe; and in general we need the help of the gift in deciding whether that correspondence is present in our actions or not. But the essential is to learn more and more to live all our lives, all our moments, in God's presence, to keep always close to God.

Here we come inevitably upon the question of technique. You will find, in many modern or relatively modern textbooks of the ascetic or mystical life, a detailed program, a more or less elaborate mechanism whose purpose is to train the mind and will to this fidelity to the Presence, but which may well repel some seekers precisely because of its studied elaboration, its air of scientific and self-conscious technique. "Is this the freedom of the sons of God," they may say. "And can love grow in this chilly atmosphere of formalism and constraint?"

The answer, for them, may well be no. We should remember that this sort of method is, in the main, a product of the particular period to which it was suited; there are undoubtedly some to whom it is still not only useful but necessary — unless they have these props and a clearly defined structure, they feel at a loss — but there are others for whom it would be disastrous, in this as in any other matter, because it would stifle them: the necessity of adhering to these set plans would be simply a worry and a distraction, and so would defeat its own purpose. For these, there are the simpler ways of the older tradition, and they need look no farther. It would be terrible to try to force oneself to obey an unsuitable technique, evolved in a particular period, under the impression that it was the one and only path to perfection: there are many mansions. . . .[102]

The essential is to learn to live in God's presence, to make love the background of all thought, desire, and action; we need the help of the gift to show us how best we, with our particular temperament and equipment, are to do it.

Knowledge directs us in prayer

The same is true of our private prayer; and this is the fourth way in which we need the gift. People sometimes suppose that mental prayer means, in practice, making use of the elaborate meditations provided in some modern books, with their sections and subsections, their rigid framework within which the mind, imagination, and will have their carefully allotted and carefully circumscribed part to play. You must not think that this is the only way. They are again the product of a particular period in the Church's history. They will be useful to some, no doubt, but a positive hindrance to others.

The older way consisted in the use of a book to turn the mind and heart to God and make prayer easy; and the use of

[102] John 14:2.

the book accordingly ceased when, and for as long as, its purpose was fulfilled. Many people will find that without a book, or without some very simple framework to which they can return when their attention has wandered, they will be lost and apt to find that their time of prayer has been one long distraction. Others may quite soon come to the stage at which they no longer need a book at all because it would, in fact, keep them from their union of heart and mind with God. The gift of knowledge should help us to avoid throwing away, out of laziness, a habit of formal meditation which is useful to us, and to avoid clinging to it, through lack of courage, when it is really a hindrance.

And what should we meditate on? Here again people are sometimes tyrannized by convention. There is no need to suppose that we must have some vast and grandiose subject for our thoughts: speculative theology must be turned into prayer, but there is no reason why prayer should be turned into speculative theology. Be simple. Anything that will make *real* to you the life and personality of our Lord (real in the sense of direct awareness instead of knowledge by hearsay or reading); anything that will bring home to you the indwelling of God in the soul and His presence in all His creatures; anything that will help you to see morality in terms of religion: all these things and many others can be the stuff out of which you make your prayer. And the more simply you handle them, the better.

You should not be afraid of meditating on ordinary things, if you can learn to see in these ordinary things not only the purposes but also the presence of God. Learn, for example, to see the symbolism in things, and not only your immediate prayer but your whole life will be immeasurably enriched.

Knowledge assures us of God's abiding presence

In these thoughts about the gift of knowledge, we are close to the third beatitude. For they who mourn are they who, in their attitude toward creatures, have achieved identity of will with God, and so have learned to use creatures not as a distraction from Him but as a way to Him and as a part of their love of Him.

It is the same whether you think of your attitude toward men and women and all creatures in themselves or whether you think of the use of created methods of coming to God: you need the gift of knowledge precisely to enable you to be of the company of those who mourn, substituting the generous love of creatures for comfort-seeking, or refusing to let a preoccupation with methods be an obstacle between you and the End. For in all these things alike, that is, in the last resort, what the gift can do: it can give an abiding sense of the abiding Presence in all things, so that at all moments and in all circumstances, you start from the conviction: "I *know* that my Redeemer liveth";[103] and on that knowledge you act and live.

[103] Job 19:25.

C. The Sacrament of this Beatitude

Penance

And Jesus alone remained, and the woman standing in the midst. Then Jesus lifting up Himself said to her: "Woman, where are they that accused thee? Hath no man condemned thee?" Who said: "No man, Lord." And Jesus said: "Neither will I condemn thee. Go, and now sin no more."[104]

We have been considering the fundamental Christian paradox: you must love *nothing* but God, or you insult your Maker; you must love *all* things, or you insult their Maker. And perhaps now the fact that it is only an apparent paradox is becoming clear.

We might say that the key to the whole problem is the omnipresence of God. "He sees God aright who sees Him in all things"; and he sees things aright who sees God's presence within them. The burden of what the men of prayer have to tell us in this connection is just this: if you fail to see God in things, then you fail to see the things themselves; and in consequence, if you love them, you are not really loving the things themselves but a part of them. And when you isolate this partial vision, and love it, you tend to make your love a

[104] John 8:9-11.

form of self-love — you tend to love things for what they can give you, you, and always you — and so indeed you set yourself up against God, and indeed creatures are a stumbling-block for you.

But if, on the other hand, you realize that God is "all in all,"[105] that He is what is inmost in things as well as what is infinitely apart from them, and that they are meant precisely to bring you to know Him — the visible things, St. Paul tells us, are meant precisely to teach us to see the invisible[106] — and if, therefore, you learn to love things not partially but wholly, then indeed you love all things. And you love them more passionately for loving them wholly, but at the same time, you love nothing but God. There is no rivalry; there is only the all-inclusive universality of the divine love itself.

We need Penance when we fail to love properly

This is the ideal; and for most of us it remains a faraway, seemingly unattainable ideal. It is so easy to forget the Presence, to isolate things from their own wholeness, and so either to idolize them or to batten on them. That is why, when we consider our attitude toward created things, we have need of sorrow and repentance: not because we have loved excessively, but because we have not loved sufficiently; we have been selfish, and so have not loved aright.

And so it is natural for us to go on to think of the healing sacrament which can redeem the past and give us hope and

[105] Eph. 1:23.
[106] Rom. 1:20.

renewal of strength for the future. All is not lost because hitherto we have failed; and if we want to see the mercy of God in the fullness of its patience, we can see it here, and be humbled and glad. It is never too late to call upon the gentle forgivingness of God: there is more joy in Heaven over one sinner doing penance than over ninety-nine just who need not penance.[107] It is never too late.

But the mercy goes farther even than that: we can never turn again too often. We are to be forgiven, not seven times, but till seventy times seven — as often as we repent.[108]

Penance administers justice and judgment

The sacrament of Penance is, first of all, a tribunal for the administering of justice and judgment. This aspect of it is essential: it means that we must approach it with the humility of confessed criminals, and that we regard punishment as our due. It means that we have to be careful to confess explicitly the exact nature and number of our grave sins — and this we should do briefly and clearly, and without making excuses or wrapping things up in many words. It means, too, that it is right to mention venial sins, at least in general. And all this discipline of self-examination and consciousness of the demands of justice is part of the purpose of the sacrament.

But we see it in its fullness when we remember, having all this in mind, that it is Christ our Lord who is the Judge, and when we remember His words to the poor woman whom the

[107] Luke 15:7.
[108] Cf. Matt. 18:21-22.

Jews were about to stone for her sin.[109] If we remember that He is never shocked or incredulous of the depths to which we can sink, and never harsh except to those who are convinced of their own sinlessness, then we shall not be tempted to let fineness of conscience (in which we grow with the growth of prayer and love) degenerate into meticulousness, anxious fear, and scrupulosity. How terrible it is when people allow their confession to be a cause of endless worry to them, when its whole purpose is to bring them back to God and His peace, to renew their courage and strength, and to set them again to live the life of love and joy.

Penance heals and fortifies

This is indeed the first thing we need to understand about the sacrament: it is not a question of simply ridding the soul of ugly marks which sin has made upon it. In the first place, that is to misunderstand the nature of sin.

If we must think of it in terms of a metaphor, let us think rather of the curing of a disease: we are lucky if a cure takes away every vestige of the disease, and leaves behind no weakness of constitution, no tendency to fall a victim to it again. Similarly we cannot normally expect that the forgiveness of

[109] Compare the scene in the synagogue at the very beginning of our Lord's public life when He read to them the words of Isaiah: "The spirit of the Lord is upon me. Wherefore he hath anointed me to preach the gospel to the *poor*: he hath sent me to *heal* the contrite of heart, to preach *deliverance* to the captive and *sight* to the blind, to *set at liberty* them that are *bruised*, to preach the acceptable year of the Lord and the day of reward." And He said to them: "This day is fulfilled this Scripture in your ears" (Luke 4:18-19, 21).

our sins will remove completely the tendency to evil choice which our own sins have made habitual in us.

On the other hand, the sacrament has a second and very positive purpose: it is concerned not only to redeem the past but to fortify us for the future. It is concerned to restore us to God and to His Church, and also to increase our unity with Him and His Church. It is not only healing but upbuilding.

We do well to see this second purpose of the sacrament in the light of the secular struggle of good and evil which we have been considering. Here as elsewhere, the life and power of God in us have more than a merely private purpose: they are given primarily to restore *this* man, *this* woman, to oneness with God. But the oneness has its social responsibility; the healing and strengthening are intended not least to empower them to help in the redemptive activity of Christ in healing and restoring the world. "Go, and now sin no more" is not only a negative command and encouragement: it means, too, "Go now, and by being yourself thus filled with the light and the life, help others to come to the light and the life, for that is your vocation as a Christian reclaimed."

God can turn our sins to good

Again we must see in this more than a giving back of life and power in general. It is not just an abrogation of the past in order to be strong and effective in the future: it is a giving of strength and effectiveness *through* the failures of the past. Even sin has its redemptive purpose; even our own personal sins can be turned to good, and are meant to be turned to good in our lives. The shame and sorrow increase the sense of sin, and the realization of the endless patience of God increases humility and wonder. These are part of that process of going down to the depths, so that there we may learn to be poor and meek, and to mourn, and so that then we may be comforted and turned into strong and fearless instruments of God's purposes.

We may not sin in order to understand — that way, the sense of sin would grow weaker and weaker within us instead of stronger — but having sinned, we can use our shame in order to understand: it is part of the deepening influence of suffering in general.

Penance should bring us peace

But we shall not use this thing as we ought, we shall not turn evil to good as we ought, unless we can find peace in the midst of shame, and joy in the midst of sorrow. If our sins cause us to be always worried and anxious, if our problems make us brood, make us introspective and scrupulous, then we defeat this part of the purpose of the sacrament.

The priest is not only judge, but also guide and pastor: you must not expect him to do all your thinking and willing for you, but you are right to ask him for help and enlightenment when you have problems you cannot solve for yourself. And when you have thus reached a conclusion or been given a ruling, you must cease altogether to worry; you must keep yourself, at all costs, from going back again and again over the old ground, worrying over the possible insufficiency of past confessions or past advice or past decisions. (Yes, there are times when things you thought too lightly of in the past appear to you in something more like their true colors; in such cases, you do well to take them again, at least silently in your heart, to God. But that is a very different thing from the endless circlings of the scrupulous mind.)

"Go, and now sin no more": it is final; it is the password to freedom: the only thing that remains is to take up the labor of life as a labor of love, expiation, and joy.

We must avoid self-complacency

On the other hand, we must remember always the condition of all forgiveness and restoration: "as we forgive them that trespass against us."[110] The confessional is no place for the self-complacent. It is better to be a sinner and recognize the fact with humility and sorrow than to avoid all spectacular wrongdoing and be complacent about it. Compare our Lord's attitude toward the poor woman with His attitude toward the Pharisees.

We must never allow ourselves to talk or think about "sinners" unless we have two things very clearly in mind: first, that we mean those who, objectively speaking, are terribly estranged from God and forgetful of Him, but this is not to imply that, where subjective guilt is concerned, we think they are necessarily in as bad a plight as ourselves; and secondly, that it is no false assumption of humility but a statement of hard fact when we say "pray for *us* sinners" — and that it is a good thing to say it when we have these others in mind. With those conditions fulfilled, it is, of course, not only a good thing but a duty to pray for those who have had less opportunity

[110] Cf. Matt. 6:12.

perhaps than we, and who perhaps, had they had as much grace, would have made better use of it.

But we might well pause here a moment to think over the easily unnoticed ways in which we can be self-complacent by being superior. St. Augustine remarks on the stealthy way in which pride can creep in without our noticing it and destroy what would otherwise have been good deeds. To be intolerant of other people's weaknesses, forgetting our own; to give way to the temptation to show other people up; to fall into the self-deception of criticizing in other people the faults we suffer from ourselves — sometimes it is possible to find out our own predominant failings by seeing what failings most arouse our indignation in other people — all these are ways of letting ourselves be conquered by self-complacency, and they can, in consequence, be very serious.

And if you are thus self-complacent, you will, of course, find it difficult to forgive others their trespasses. But if you are poor in spirit and meek and filled with the sense of sin, and if you have learned to mourn in the sense that you are ready to accept as God's gift not only the enjoyable things He sends but the trying ones (and those trials in particular which come from the angularities, the thoughtlessness, the ingratitude, and the spite of other people), and to accept them in the realization that indeed you deserve nothing better, then indeed you find it easy to forgive. Rather, you scarcely think in terms of forgiving, for you do not think in terms of injuries. And in and by this mourning, too, you will be comforted: for through it you will learn to see more and more clearly and deeply the omnipresence of God, and to achieve a deeper identity of your will with His.

We must avoid pettiness

This is a context in which we shall be well advised to keep our eyes open for the petty sins which, precisely because they are so petty, can be dangerous and grave. The sense of sin teaches us that we are each responsible for all, because we are a family; it teaches us to ask ourselves how far the failure of the family is due to our own failure; and it reminds us that family squabbles tend to be petty, and that just because they are petty, they can be a poison in the family life.

The sacrament of Penance should make us humble and glad and large-hearted: humble because of the sense of sin; glad because of the renewal of life and freedom; and large-hearted because pettiness keeps us self-centered and isolated from God, but life and freedom are given to us so that we may serve God and His family and live in God's love of His family. But we have to be humble and glad and large-hearted precisely *in* our mourning; if we obey the Spirit, we shall find these things *in* the discipline of the confessional and the sorrow that attends it. We learn these family virtues because, through the power of the sacrament and the gift of the Spirit, we can learn to choose discomfort.

And so the family ties bind us more strongly and our love grows, and the negative side of penance turns quickly into the positive, and we learn gradually the key to the Christian paradox. We learn to love not just the utility or the pleasantness of some things for us, but the goodness and beauty of all things in themselves.

It is this idea of the growth of true love as opposed to false or partial love that gives us the clue to the Christian doctrine of mortification. To say, "Happy are they who mourn" is to say, "Happy are they who mortify themselves and take up their cross daily."[111] But we go astray and forget the beatitude unless we remember that mortification must be based on a real love and awareness of things within the framework of the love of God and His will, and that detachment in general is not insensitivity but love — real love, the love that is defined and measured by Love.

We have to be ready to choose discomfort when Love demands it. And of course Love does demand it, first of all because the self-seeking which is so deeply rooted in us is an offense against love.

Suffering helps us in three ways

The first use to which we must put suffering in general and mortification in particular is known as asceticism: training ourselves to be obedient to God by denying ourselves, more than is strictly necessary, the indulgence of our own desires, so that flesh may become less rebellious to spirit and the whole being may, therefore, be free for its service of God.

Secondly, suffering helps us to expiate: we right the balance of justice which our sins have upset, by voluntarily suffering something for the love of God. And indeed this function of suffering need not be confined to satisfying for our own sins merely, but may have its share in helping to expiate for the sins of the world. Nor may we allow ourselves to think that, as is sometimes said, this whole idea of expiation by suffering is a

[111] Matt. 16:24; Mark 8:34; Luke 9:23.

practical assertion that pain is something good in itself, something in which God delights for its own sake.

There is a deep-rooted instinct in us which makes us feel that those who, by cruelty, have made others suffer should be made to suffer themselves, and it is an instinct which is supported by theology. To be cruel is to increase the evil in the world, to increase the total of violent self-assertion; and it must be put right by a corresponding act in the opposite direction, an act in which the proud self is humbled and made to accept what it once rejected, that is, the existence of an absolute standard — of justice, goodness, and love — to which man must conform.

So it was that the total self-assertion of the world in defiance of God was expiated by the total self-dedication, the total obedience, of Christ; and it is in this act of expiation that those who suffer now may share — and, if they are living in the love of God, will want to share.

For, thirdly, it is part of love to want to share in the sufferings of those we love (just as the fact of sharing in others' sufferings can cause us to love them, or to love them more). If we can grow sufficiently in the love of Christ, we shall begin to want to share in His sufferings simply because they are His sufferings, and incidentally, through this loving and redemptive pain for the world, we ourselves shall grow in our love for that world in and for Him.

Suffering can make us patient in three ways

St. James tells us that trials should be a joy to us because they are the material of patience, which he calls the "perfect work."[112] Your asceticism should make you triply patient. It should make you patient with others: with their oddities and foibles, their slowness, their weaknesses, and the injuries they do you. It should make you patient with yourself: not worrying about your lack of progress, although sorrowing over it; doing the best you can with the ordinary humble things God gives you to do, and leaving the rest to Him. And it should make you humbly patient, therefore, toward the Providence of God in every detail: learning to accept in peace and calm whatever things come to you, precisely because they come as part of that inclusive Providence — learning, therefore, more and more to care and not to care.

So the effect of mortification, of the sacrament of Penance, and of the gift of knowledge, is not to crush the personality but to free it, and to fill it with strength, peace, and joy, and thus enable it to seek God more wholeheartedly, to begin to live in His love. At the same time, it will not crush your love of creatures, but, on the contrary, will make it more real and deep. Finally, it will not withdraw you from God's family, but make you love and serve it better and better for His sake and in His sight, until at the end you can say of the whole world the words of the psalmist: "I have loved, O Lord, the beauty of Thy house, and the place where Thy glory dwelleth."[113]

[112] James 1:4.

[113] Ps. 25:8 (RSV= Ps. 26:8).

Chapter Six

Blessed are they who hunger and thirst for justice, for they shall have their fill.

Matt. 5:6

A. The Meaning of this Beatitude

Hunger for justice

Some have held that happiness consists in selfishly following the bent of the passion for wealth or pleasure or power. They are wrong, because these instincts thus isolated and so turned to evil are, on the contrary, an obstacle to happiness.

Others have thought that happiness consists in the "active life" as such, in doing rather than being. And again, they are wrong, for activity is either a *means* to happiness, or else is itself beatific only as an *overflow* of a state of being. Happiness is not, essentially, something we *have* but something we *are*, although we become what we are by doing — and by the way we suffer when suffering is given to us, and that way is itself a form of doing.

But the active life is a social life; and so this beatitude and the next tell us how we should act toward the rest of the family, first as far as justice is concerned, and secondly in regard to the qualities of soul that go beyond the bare demands of justice: generosity and mercy.

Being is more important than doing. It is wrong to think that in order to do great things for the human family, you must be endlessly occupied with external activity, and that you must be able to point to the arresting visible changes in the face of things — the institutions, the buildings, and the movements that owe their origins to you. The saints often have these things to their credit, but they achieve them almost, as it were, in spite of themselves, certainly rather as an inevitable result and expression of what they *are* than as a studied program.

Only the power that comes from inner holiness is lasting

There are always some in the world who think themselves great because their brief appearance on the stage is accompanied with much sound and fury: they have much external power, and use it to change, for a time, the face of the earth. But in reality they are as the grass that withers:[114] they go, and the upheavals they caused are at length forgotten, or figure as a tale in the textbooks of history.

The power that lives on is the real power, the inner power: the power to move mountains, to tame animals and bring them back, as St. Francis[115] did, to the human family. It is the power to charm men to holiness not merely by what is said, but by the voice that says it and the personality it expresses.

You find a hint or likeness of this power in all the really great: in the men of genius, perhaps, in the great lovers of humanity, in those who are filled with the love of a purpose greater than themselves. But you find it in its fullness in the

[114] Ps. 128:6 (RSV = Ps. 129:6).

[115] Probably St. Francis of Assisi (c. 1182-1226), founder of the Franciscan Order. — ED.

saints, whose power is more than human, since it is the life of the Spirit within them. You find it, above all, in the life of Him from whom the saints' power comes: "And Jesus returned in the *power* of the Spirit into Galilee"; "and they wondered at the *grace* that proceeded from His mouth"; "and they were astonished at His doctrine, for His speech was with *power*"; "and they talked among themselves, saying: What word is this, for with authority and *power* He commandeth the unclean spirits, and they go out?"[116]

So it was, too, that when the woman sought to be cured of the issue of blood, Jesus said, "Who hath touched my garments?" for He knew that power had gone out from Him.[117] And it is not only a power to heal the body or to give physical strength that goes forth: you look Him in the eyes or hear His voice, and you are never the same again; your whole former life is a land to which you can never return. A great Dominican, himself a man in whom there was something of this inner power, once finely said: "When our Lord calls a man a sinner, he isn't one — he used to be."

This is the power that lives on long after the one who has it has passed from the earth; for the original influence is handed on to others and to others again, and from generation to generation down the ages of the world. And perhaps those who receive of it long afterward do not know to whom originally it was due, but one day they will know, and will thank and bless him. This is the power that is real greatness. But what about the men who have lusted after power and have

[116] Luke 4:14, 22, 32, 36.

[117] Mark 5:30.

grasped at it, and made a makeshift with mere externals, and then with these means at their disposal have tortured the world? What achievement will live after them? Perhaps only this, which would never occur to them: that they have been the ignorant, unconscious instruments of a purpose far beyond their understanding, because through the suffering their lust for power has inflicted, the poor and humble and unfortunate have learned true greatness of heart.

The Commandments show us God more clearly

It is not the magnitude, or otherwise, of the work we have to do that should concern us, but the magnitude of the love with which we do it. It is a terrible mistake to suppose that if we simply carry out the Commandments externally, we have nothing to worry about. That can be no more than lip service; it can be simply self-culture, the service of the self; and it can be a form of self-complacency and the kind of practical Pelagianism[118] which thinks it can get on very well without worrying too much about its radical sinfulness and need of God.

Of course we have to try to keep the Commandments, but the essential is to try to keep them in such a way that we learn to see more and more clearly our true Center, to keep our eyes more and more on God and less and less on ourselves, and to say, "I live, now not I, but Christ liveth in me."

There are, in fact, two opposite heresies here which we have to avoid. One says: if I do right, it doesn't matter what I

[118] The heresy that holds that man is able to take the first, basic steps toward salvation by his own efforts, without the help of God's grace.

am; the other says: if I am right, it doesn't matter what I do. We have to try to live in God, to be right; but we learn to be right only through slowly and painfully trying to do right. On the other hand, if we were really living in God, then inevitably we should, as a matter of fact, do right, for we should hunger and thirst for righteousness.

Serving God requires serving others

We should hunger and thirst for the realization of God's goodness in the world. With all of our hearts, we should want that goodness to be expressed and apparent in everything in the world, and in everything that is done in the world. We should hunger and thirst for *social* justice. There can be no ivory tower for the Christian. We are a family; and we serve God — we do right — if and only if we serve Him through serving the family, whether through prayer or action.

First then, let us think of what this thirst for social justice implies. The virtue of justice causes us to "render to every man his due."[119] That is the bare minimum. Some people think they can achieve happiness by being unjust, at least in the sense of seizing what they can for themselves without consideration for the rest of the family. That way leads not to happiness but to unhappiness, because it must lead to loneliness, to isolation from God and man alike. To be happy you must think in terms of the family, and of the family as capable, through God-given power, of eventually expressing the goodness of God, the ideal shape of things.

[119] Cf. Matt. 16:27; Rom. 2:6.

Justice is the minimum requirement; but although it is the minimum, we are not to think it unimportant. Unless there is that, there can be nothing further; anything else will be poisoned and turned sour, like the grandiose philanthropy, the flourished checks, of men grown fat on sweated labor.

We must have an "insatiable desire" for justice

But the gift takes us farther than the virtue: it gives us, in St. Thomas's phrase, that "insatiable desire" for justice which you find in the saints: not merely that you do your own duty by your fellowmen, but that you are possessed by the desire to see justice done throughout the world.

Here we must return to the thought of our solidarity in sin: wherever injustice is done in the world, I am involved, I must take a share of the blame; and if I am responsible, then I must labor to redress the injustice. But I must labor according to my own particular vocation. It is not for everyone to be directly and actively engaged in the righting of social wrongs; there are other ways of sharing in the work. We can help simply by the power of prayer; we can help simply by *being*, simply by having the inner power of goodness within us.

Wherever there is injustice against men and women, there is a blind or malevolent lack of reverence for men and women. And if you are the sort of person who is possessed by the spirit of reverence, and therefore the sort of person in whom that spirit is apparent and impressive, then simply by being what you are, you recall those who come in contact with you to a sense of this form of goodness. You speak not to their minds only, but, perhaps without their realizing it, to the deep places of their hearts, the places from which the impressions of goodness are less likely to fade.

But you must help in one way or another. It is terrible when people think that a social conscience is something added on to the Christian conscience, a sort of work of supererogation. Thou shalt love thy neighbor as thyself:[120] it is the *staff* of the Christian life; and without it, there is nothing but a sham. You can never say that you fulfill the requirements of the virtue of justice and that this is sufficient: Christianity is not justice alone, but love; and it is love that the gift helps you to express. You must have the love that is an insatiable desire for justice.

The desire for justice is particularly needed today

Every time and period of the world's history calls for the desire for justice: there is always injustice between men; there is always failure to realize in the world the divine will for the world, and for this you are always bound to work and pray. But when you live in days like the present, which are filled with injustice so appalling as to be unimaginable; when the whole world is torn with the agony of men, women, and children; when, beyond and beneath the physical horrors, there is the dead weight, the stifling pall of hatred, cruelty, and brute stupidity; and when all of this is turned explicitly not only against humanity but against the Godhead, so that you have not only a failure to realize the form of goodness in the world, but a furious lust to destroy what little of that form of goodness has in fact been achieved — then indeed you need to hunger

[120] Lev. 19:18; Matt. 19:19.

and thirst for justice with insatiable desire, and you need the gift of the Spirit to save you from despair.

We must see justice in terms of God's rights

We must not think of justice only in terms of the rights of men: we must think of it primarily in terms of the rights of God, from whom all other rights are derived. Forget these, and your work for humanity is likely to degenerate into sentimentality and lead only to confusion. It is not enough to have the will to serve humanity; you must have the knowledge: you must know in what justice consists — and we have surely seen enough of man-made definitions of justice.

St. Thomas connects this beatitude with the gift of fortitude: the fortitude which expresses an insatiable desire for the respecting of *God's* rights, and which will not be deterred from fighting for those rights, no matter what may come.

Zeal for justice must manifest itself in quiet fortitude

But we have to be very careful here. This is not a question of "militant Christianity" — of stridency and vulgarity, or of an attempt to preach the Cross at the point of the bayonet. You fight for the cause of love and truth only with the weapons of love and truth. Violence is a sin against love; wanton vulgarity is a sin against truth.

The zeal for justice is meaningless unless we ourselves are just, and to be just is to do just things justly — the manner is important as well as the deed, the means as well as the end. If you want to work for justice, then you must remember the

Beatitudes: you must work in poverty of spirit and meekness of heart.

This fortitude of the saints is not a melodramatic irruption into the lives and affairs of other men and women against their will: you could almost say its keynote is a quality of quietness. The quiet refusal to betray their own integrity of mind for the sake of accommodation with their environment; the quiet refusal to swim with the current in matters of personal behavior; the quiet refusal to let fear keep them dumb when unambiguous issues arise and a declaration is expected of them at least implicitly; a quiet and humble determination to help the other members of the family when it is possible to give help with courtesy: these are the ways in which fortitude is required of us, not with loud-voiced propaganda and advertisement, and the blare of trumpets.

Yet we must not think of this work of fighting for the rights of God in the world as a question merely of opposing what is evil. It is a positive thing. It is a question of working, with insatiable desire, to build up the life of the Church: to build up the vitality of Her thought and love, the integrity and beauty of Her worship, and the universality of Her love in practice.

For all these things depend on us. The qualities are there, the power is there, for the Church is the Christ-life on earth. But in another sense, the Church is the community of the faithful, the communion of saints but also the communion of sinners; it depends on us whether the love and the power will be fully shown forth to the world. In this sense, the vitality of the Church and of Her thought and prayer depends on the vitality of our love and thought and prayer; Her worship is diminished and degraded if we play our part ill; Her love is stifled if we refuse to be filled with it and to allow it to shine forth from us to the world.

We may or may not be called upon, like the martyrs, to die for the Church, but we are quite certainly called upon to *live* for the Church, and that requires fortitude enough, and zeal for justice. You must never be led by self-love into sinning against justice to men, or into deceiving yourself about what justice, in fact, demands. You must never let the love of comfort or esteem lead you into frightened silence when you should speak.

You are to be as tenacious of God's rights as you are carefree about your own. You are to serve the Church — the life, thought, worship, and love of the Church — with insatiable desire for the beauty of God's house. And you are to do all this no matter what inconvenience, suffering, or sorrow it may bring. That is what hunger and thirst for justice implies; and that is the sort of active life, the God-centered life, which will lead to Heaven.

Zeal for justice requires meekness and self-denial

This beatitude, then, is the corollary of meekness, and the elucidation of what is meant by *mourning*. You must try to be carefree about your own well-being, your own dignity, and the esteem of men, so as to be able to turn your mind to the needs of the world and the rights of God. You cannot be zealous unless you are first meek.

But equally you cannot be zealous unless you have learned to be among those who mourn: unless the idea of discomfort and suffering for the sake of love has lost its terrors for you and is something you welcome gladly — or at least unless you are ready to face the terrors. And even then the terror that is met with fortitude and endured with love will not quench the soul's joy.

Zeal for justice brings comfort even in this life

They shall have their fill. It is more, St. Thomas says, to be comforted in the kingdom than merely to have and possess it; but it is more, again, to have your fill, to have the fullness of comfort which leaves no sorrow unassuaged. There is a sense, indeed, in which this fullness of comfort can only come after suffering: if you hunger and thirst for justice, and suffer for it, your labors and your suffering have their redemptive purpose and effect. You may in this life be despised and rejected as was a greater than you, but you will have helped and healed many directly, and perhaps more indirectly than you can ever count. And the time will come when this your particular family will gather about you and thank you and bless you and lead you to God to beg Him to thank you too, and then indeed your joy will be filled.

But even in the midst of the sorrows, you will have your fullness of comfort in another sense if you thus suffer gladly for the love of God and in the power of the Spirit: first, because God does not wait until we have realized what we have done before thanking us for our service of Him; and secondly because you will work not with the thought of reward but with the joy in giving which is the essence of love. Everything that you do and give with insatiable zeal, everything that with fortitude you suffer or withstand will be a gift of love, and to give gifts in this way is not to look for a reward but to have it.

Zeal for justice depends on humility

Still, this ability to hunger and thirst for justice depends so much upon humility, and therefore upon the sense of sin, that we may perhaps be wise to return finally to the thought of the incomprehensible courtesy and gentleness of God, who will thank those who bring Him these gifts even though they are able to bring them only because He has given them first. You give Him fidelity, but it is His gift to you; you give Him courage and endurance, but they come from Him; you give Him the zeal which is love, but it is only a shared likeness of the eternal Love. When we think long and deeply of these humbling facts, we can hope to begin to be strong without being hard, to be brave without being arrogant, to hunger and thirst for justice and not for our own glory.

And then we may think of the immense fertility of this God-given inner power, the power that heals and comforts and restores: first spreading its roots wider and wider in the soil of the present; and thereafter making life a different, a new thing, perhaps, for unnumbered multitudes from generation to generation down through the ages of the world. We can think of it thus as the seed in our Lord's own simile, the seed growing secretly, with the quietness of true zeal, and so turning, in the end, into the mighty tree in which the birds of the air can come and build their nests — even the world of nature being thus, in degree, restored and healed — a tree of life, flowering into Paradise.[121]

[121] Cf. Matt. 13:31-32; Rev. 2:7.

B. The Gift of this Beatitude

Lukewarmness and the gift of fortitude

Such as I love I rebuke and chastise. Be zealous therefore, and do penance. Behold, I stand at the gate and knock. If any man shall hear my voice and open to me the door, I will come in to him and sup with him, and he with me. To him that shall overcome I will give to sit with me in my throne. . . . He that hath an ear, let him hear what the Spirit saith to the churches.[122]

The preceding lines from Revelation give us a sort of summary of what we have been thinking of so far. Before the birth to the new life, there must be the death of the evil self, and the death is necessarily a process of rebuke and chastisement, a doing of penance; and the doing of this penance, this turning from the false center to the true, is not to be accomplished without zeal, without the hunger and thirst for justice that we have just been considering.

We might recall, too, the words of an earlier preacher of repentance, to remind ourselves that this process is not purely a private affair of our own. St. John the Baptist, when asked, "What then shall we do?" tells his listeners, "He that hath two coats, let him give to him that hath none; and he that hath

[122] Rev. 3:19-22.

meat, let him do in like manner";[123] we save ourselves through serving our family.

But this process is not something that we can do; it is something that can be done in us, if we will. "I stand at the gate and knock"; "hear what the Spirit saith to the churches." If we are to have the life and the power of God, it can only be by the gift of God; it is for us to be docile. But then, if we are zealous in our docility, if our hunger and thirst for justice are intense enough to make us wholly obedient to the voice of the Spirit, and if we have the fortitude to overcome the evil self in us and to labor for the overcoming of the spirit of evil in the world, which is our family, then we shall be invited to the table; we shall be given to sit in the throne.

Let us think, first of all, of the opposite of zeal, which we call lukewarmness, and then turn to study more in detail the virtue and the gift of fortitude.

Lukewarmness prevents us from receiving God's life and power

You find lukewarmness dealt with in the third chapter of Revelation: "I know thy works, that thou art neither cold nor hot. I would thou wert cold or hot. But because thou art lukewarm and neither cold nor hot, I will begin to vomit thee out of my mouth."[124]

You think, at first sight, that this is unfair; that it must surely be better to be lukewarm than to be downright cold,

[123] Luke 3:10-11.

[124] Rev. 3:15-16.

better to be indifferent than to hate. But hatred at least implies an interest; there is at least a possibility that some chastisement, which plunges the soul down to the depths, may open our eyes and then perhaps our hearts. Perfect indifference is the greater insult; and the more irremediable state of soul.

And it is worth noting that lukewarmness is a state of soul, not a sinful act: a state of soul like the physical condition we call being run down, a state in which you may catch anything. It is caused, first of all, by an inattention to venial sin. The area of what we regard as negligible increases; we begin to think of grave sins as being, at least in our case, unimportant peccadilloes; and where it is a question not of refraining from evil but of doing good, our conscience becomes less and less exigent, our duties appear to us less and less exorbitant: we first develop a skill in arguing ourselves out of obvious duties, and then, as time goes on, we cease to bother to argue. And meanwhile a hard shell of indifference is forming around the spirit, and stifling it, until in the end it may well prove impervious to the influence of God and man alike, impregnable. He stands at the gate and knocks, but there is no reply.

And that is essentially what lukewarmness means: it is not using, not receiving, the life and power of God; in the latter stages, it is a positive resistance to the offered power, a positive refusal to listen to the voice of the Spirit. We have no further interest in the life, the power, and the voice: we are bored. So at the end, we find we are in Hell — and it is this that makes the eternity of Hell, and the fact of Hell at all, an obvious inevitability, given free will: we have turned ourselves into people of this sort, and people of this sort are precisely people who *cannot* turn again because they have made it impossible.

And being unable to turn again, they *cannot* live with God; they are eternally, irredeemably, enclosed in their shell of boredom.

Sometimes God, in His mercy, recalls us, just in time. We can never ask forgiveness too late or too often. But if we are given the mercy, and turn again, it must be as a child that we turn: in poverty, in meekness, and in the humility and shame of self-knowledge. Otherwise our fortitude will be a sham, a passing parade, and we shall sink back again. "Go, and now sin no more" means "Go, and now in *my* power, *my* strength, *my* courage, sin no more."

The virtue of fortitude gives us the strength of soul to do what we ought to do in spite of grave perils or obstacles — mastering fear on the one hand and controlling rashness on the other, for both of these can injure the work to be done. St. Thomas treats of four minor virtues which lead us to act in the same sort of way in regard to less-serious obstacles which may confront us: the virtues of great-heartedness, magnificence, patience, and perseverance.

Great-heartedness is not daunted by the magnitude of works

Great-heartedness leads us to undertake great and arduous works in every kind of virtue without taking fright at their *magnitude*. As a Christian virtue, it goes, of course, side by side with humility: it is what enables us to say, "I can do all things" only "in Him who strengtheneth me." So, because of its strength, it conquers the pusillanimity which is afraid to do great deeds even though they are within one's power, and which takes refuge in false modesty. Because of its humility, it conquers the presumption which tries to do things beyond its powers. It conquers the vainglory which loves to be praised either for things not in themselves praiseworthy, or, as St. Thomas shrewdly remarks, by those who are incapable of mature judgment. It conquers the vanity which takes to itself alone the honor and glory of what is done, instead of thanking God. It conquers the ambition which seeks self-glorification, and replaces it with the true ambition which wants to use every talent and do great deeds in obedience to God and for love of Him.

Magnificence does not count the cost of doing good

Magnificence is the virtue which will not allow great works for God to be impeded by fear of great *expenditure*, and so it is a species of this greatness of heart. And although this is primarily a virtue which concerns those who have the disposal of riches, it is to be found also — and how magnificently — in the poor, who will cheerfully spend the savings of many years in providing a feast for a daughter's wedding or a son's homecoming.

This is the greatness of soul which overcomes both senseless extravagance and niggardliness. It is an expression of that spirit of poverty and detachment which we were thinking of before: it is the expression of humility. We are only God's stewards. He gives us things so that we may serve the family, and for this reason, we must not be wasteful, but we must not be miserly either. Sometimes there are magnificent gifts we can give directly to God, like Mary the sinner with her box of precious spikenard;[125] but there is always the family, there are always the poor, and when we give magnificently to them, we give to God.

Patience and perseverance enable us to overcome evil, fatigue, and boredom

Patience is the strength to endure present *evils inflicted* by others without being unduly disturbed and abandoning the work in hand: the nagging criticisms, the lack of sympathy and help, the incomprehension, and the derision which can make it so hard to go on. And with it goes what St. Paul calls longanimity: the ability not to be discouraged because the good aimed at is so far off and the road so long.

And perseverance, in its turn, has a similar function: to enable us to go on with the task given to us in spite of the *fatigue* and boredom that attend a job that must be taken up again day after day and week after week until it is done.

The gift of fortitude gives us confidence in God

It is at this point that we come upon the necessity of the *gift* of fortitude. For the virtue, says St. Thomas, gives a man courage and strength to *sustain* all dangers and difficulties; but the gift goes farther than that; it instills in the soul a *confidence* that all dangers and difficulties will be *overcome*.

This, indeed, is something beyond the power of human nature to perform, for many enterprises are interrupted before

[125] John 12:3.

their completion by the hand of death; but it is not beyond the power of the Spirit, who brings men to eternal life, the completion of all work, and the deliverance from all dangers. So it is the gift of fortitude that you see in the joy and gaiety of the martyrs, who have *confidence* that their torments will not cause them to falter and rob them of eternal life, but, on the contrary, will take them, through the power of the Spirit, straight to the arms of God.

And we can see the same sort of confidence and quiet joy in all the works of the saints. What they build, they build steadfastly and in tranquillity, and neither apparent failures during their lives nor the advent of death can dismay them or cause them to lose their confidence in the final outcome; for all their building is in the hand of God, and in Him they trust, with all the child's unquestioning trust that what his father has begun he will see to its conclusion.

So, to hear what the Spirit says, to accept His guidance, is to work with all one's strength in the present, but to leave the future in quiet and humble confidence to Him. It is to be zealous, to have the strength of will of the man; but it is also to be filled, through the power of the Spirit, with the freshness and spontaneity, the zest and the enthusiasm, of the child.

Fortitude increases fervor

There is a tendency in any age like our own, a *fin du siècle* period when the world has grown stale, for people to be ready to argue and discuss and perhaps accept a conclusion to the discussion, abstractly, but never to let this conclusion affect the conduct of real life. Perhaps it is the vice especially of the "intellectual." Fortitude can give us precisely the motive force which is lacking: it rejuvenates — we have the water of re-birth — and in its power we can have the zest and vigor and single-mindedness of the young.

"Be zealous." But we have to remember that this is not necessarily, and certainly not primarily, a question of doing more and more things; it is a question of loving more and more deeply and intensely, and therefore of doing the things we do with more and more fervor. An increase in the quantity and extent of our work will no doubt follow, for if we are filled with love, we shall be impelled to give always more and more; that is the logical order.

"The zeal of thy house hath eaten me up":[126] when that is true of us, we shall not be lukewarm in our outward works, nor run the risk of their being hollow, useless, and perhaps harmful. And let us give full value to the word *house*: it is first of all the worship of God that is in question. But the world is the Lord's and the fullness thereof;[127] that, too, is His house; that, too, we must serve with zeal and fortitude if we want it to be really Him that we serve, for inasmuch as we do it at His call to the least of these little ones, and only so, we do it unto Him.[128]

The prayer of petition requires fortitude

This zealous care for the house of God and our family suggests some thoughts about the prayer of petition. We need

[126] Ps. 68:10 (RSV = Ps. 69:9).
[127] Ps. 88:12 (RSV = Ps. 89:11).
[128] Cf. Matt. 25:40.

to pray the prayer of awe; we need to pray the prayer of reverent filial piety and love; but we need also the *fiducia mentis*, the boundless trust, which the gift of fortitude gives us — the almost arrogant prayer of petition of the saints. There is nothing that love cannot ask for, if it is part of love to ask for it. The faith that moves mountains is expressed in the prayer that moves mountains. "Ask the Father anything in my name . . ."[129]

It is part of the humility which says, "I can do all things" to be able to pray for all things. And indeed you have in this boundlessly trusting prayer of the saints the whole essence of Christian fortitude. The highest exercise of strength, maturity, and self-possession and the highest degree of leaning on the power of God meet in the prayer which is at once a total dependence on the divine will and a prelude to heroic initiative and heroic labor.

The prayer of petition is compatible with Providence

What are we to pray for? We are *bound* to ask for all we need, and for all the needs of those dependent on us — not in detail, of course, but at least in general terms: Give us our daily bread.[130] We are *right* to ask for what we want, but always with the condition "not my will but Thine be done"; always, too, with the condition, implicit at least, "if it is for the good of the family."

It is this conditional quality of all prayer of petition that answers the difficulties of those who feel that it must be a

[129] John 16:23.

[130] Matt. 6:11.

pointless and insulting attempt to alter the almighty Providence of God. Since everything is already determined, what is the use of this prayer, what is the use of trying to alter the divine decree?

The answer is that this prayer does not attempt to alter the divine decree: we pray not *against* the framework of Providence but *within* it. We pray because prayer is one of the forces, the energies, which govern events in the world — as many other nonmaterial things, modes of thought, will, and desire, govern events in the world. We pray because, in the design of Providence, this prayer may be foreordained to contribute to the bringing about in the world of this event rather than that.

So we pray always with the *fiat voluntas Tua*, "Thy will be done"; and if the immediate object of the prayer is not to be granted to us, still the prayer can never be pointless or wholly unfulfilled, because every prayer which is thus conditional is a prayer for the good of God's family and, in that sense, will be heard.

Fortitude allows us to persevere in prayer

But to pray conditionally is not to pray half-heartedly. We must have the gift of fortitude to go on praying for what we need and for what the family needs when the prayer is not immediately heard — for perseverance in prayer, too, may be part of Providence. And if we use to the full this gift of fortitude and we love God and the family enough, then we shall do more than ask: we shall almost demand, and our demands will be heard; for one of the great joys of love is to be able to give when asked, and God is not niggardly in love.

It is this certainty of God's will to listen, this *fiducia* of fortitude, that you find in the saints; it is this that you find so fully expressed in the words of the Mother of God at Cana, when she does not even turn her wish into a request, but leaves it as a simple statement: "They have no wine."[131]

This takes us beyond the prayer of awe and the prayer of piety, nearer to the prayer which is proper to the children of God: the simple, loving, trustful expression of need and desire.

We can acquire fortitude through prayer

"If any man shall hear my voice and open to me . . ." We need this prayer of petition not least *in order that* we may have fortitude in our lives; we shall not hear the voice unless our ears are accustomed to the air through which it breathes and have learned to listen by learning to pray.

Prayer and fortitude are interactive therefore: we need fortitude to persevere in prayer in spite of every obstacle of laziness, distraction, aridity, and apparent ineffectiveness; we need prayer to give us fortitude by giving us the constant sense of the presence of God and His Providence. And then, if we learn to acquire this fortitude in prayer and in action alike, if we learn to hear the voice and open the door, to be zealous and turn again and do penance and overcome, then He will see to it that we have, deep within us, the joyous sense that the work will be brought to its proper conclusion, for He Himself will be with us and guide and sustain our hands. He will come in to us and sup with us, and we with Him, and we shall have our fill.

[131] John 2:3.

C. The Sacrament of this Beatitude

The Holy Eucharist

He that eateth my flesh and drinketh my blood
abideth in me, and I in him.[132]

He will come in to us and sup with us, and we with Him. This is not only a future beatitude that is offered to us, but a present reality which we can have, if we will, day by day.

And if we are thinking of our need of fortitude and of the courage to go on day by day with the work given to us, then it is natural to think also of this sacrament of the daily bread, which is intended precisely to give us the daily renewal of strength for the daily task, and to fill us with the energy — with the life and power — which will make us do great things for God.

"He that eateth my flesh and drinketh my blood hath everlasting life":[133] the tense is the present; you have the life here and now, and so you are filled with power. *Et ambulavit in fortitudine cibi illius:* "He walked in the strength" — the

[132] John 6:57 (RSV = John 6:56).
[133] John 6:55 (RSV = John 6:54).

fortitude — "of that food forty days and forty nights, unto the mount of God."[134]

The Eucharist unites us with Christ

But again, the power implies a social responsibility: we are empowered to live a family life; and this greatest of the sacraments is precisely the sacrament of *unity*. The Christian's journey is not meant to be a lonely one. But to achieve a family life, you must avoid two opposite dangers: you must avoid individualism, the private search for a private sanctification; and you must equally avoid totalitarianism, the idea of an imposed uniformity which is the destruction of the individual. The family of God is meant to be a unity, but a unity of real living men and women, really bringing something — a unique creative gift — to the common life.

The Lord's Supper is the sacrament of unity because its first purpose is to cause us to live in the life of Christ, to be one with Him; but also because its effect should be to forge anew the unity of men with one another, and thence to restore something of the unity of all creatures, since it is the whole of creation which it sanctifies.

The Mass involves all creation

The Mass is, first of all, a sacrifice. That is the first way in which it fulfills a universal instinct and desire of mankind. Sacrifice is a necessity because it is part of the nature of the

[134] 3 Kings 19:8 (RSV = 1 Kings 19:8).

creature to express its dependence on its Creator: to fail to say, "In comparison with You, I am nothing because all I have and all I am is from You" is to do violence to one's nature; it is to attempt — as Adam attempted — to cease to be a creature at all. The essence of sacrifice is this inward offering of the self.

For what reason, then, do we use these material things to express an inward offering? It is because we are not spirit but body-spirit: the use of material things is our natural mode of expression.

But there is more than that. This sacrifice is the summary and the fulfillment of all the sacrifices of all the races of the world because the thing offered is Him who is All in all. The self is offered, yes; but it is offered as a part of something much greater, as part of the self-offering of the Infinite made flesh, and therefore as part of the self-offering of the whole world included in that infinite act of offering.

You go to Mass to offer yourself to God, but you are part of the self-offering of the whole Church in Christ, who redeems and sanctifies the whole world; and so you take with you the whole of creation, for "the whole of creation is in travail even till now," waiting to be "delivered from the servitude of corruption, into the liberty of the glory of the children of God."[135] So with the bread and wine of the sacrifice, you offer the earth and the fullness thereof, the things that grow and are meant to minister to man's needs and give him joy; in the song and gesture and movement of the Mass, and in the stones and glass, the carvings and paintings that house and adorn it, you

[135] Rom. 8:22, 21.

offer all the arts of man. The symbols of the evangelists are there to remind you that the beasts, too, share in the travail of creation and must share in its restoration.

Everything in your own life must be offered in order to be cleansed and transformed by being caught up into this single cosmic act of worship; but everything in the world must be offered, too, and for the same purpose.

The Mass transcends time

The sacrifice of the Mass is one and the same as that of the Cross: you are taking part in Calvary. Christ is not simply a historical figure, now gone from the earth. The Mass *is* the sacrifice of Calvary because Priest and Victim are in each the same; it is one and the same Christ who offers and is offered. Christ is with us in the world today.

But, moreover, when you take part in the Mass, the curtains of time are rolled back and you step into the eternal present because the Mass transcends time: you are taking part in an eternal act of will. The agony, the way of the Cross, and the death on the Cross: these are events in the past; but they are the physical and historical expression of an act of will of a Man who is also the God in whom there is no change. The mode changes; the substance remains the same.

Your own self-offering and your offering of the world which is your family are raised to infinity because they are included in this single act of self-offering of a Victim who is divine. So in the offering, all things are made one. This is the second way in which the Mass fulfills the universal instinct and desire of mankind.

The Mass makes Christ sacramentally present

But the Mass is also a sacrament, the means whereby this redemptive act is made operative day by day in the world. Creation waits for delivery from the servitude of corruption, waits for the liberty of the glory of the children of God. This is not a forlorn hope, but an expectancy, precisely because of the Mass, which is the center of the whole sacramental system, of that economy whereby the life and the power are given to souls and so spread abroad on the earth. It is through the Mass above all that Christ, the sacrificial Christ, is with us.

God is everywhere; He is All in all. But here you have a new, redemptive presence: it is the redeeming Christ, who, through the Mass, is still with the earth to save, heal, and bless it; who, through the Mass, can walk again the lanes and fields of England; who, through the Mass, visits the slums and tenements, and weeps now over the battlefields and the bombed cities as once over Jerusalem.[136]

And the presence of this redeeming love and power, this promise of liberty and glory to a world in servitude is the third way in which the Mass fulfills the desire of mankind. For the power is able, if only we will use it, not only to transform the squalors and sufferings begotten of injustice into spiritual splendor, but still more to overcome in the end the spirit of evil which produces the squalors.

We shall not see the Mass aright unless we realize that sacrament and sacrifice are one: we must not separate the joy of the supper from the sacrificial death.

[136] Luke 19:41.

The Mass is both an offering and a receiving

Let us think, first of all, of the lesson of the structure of the Mass. There is the great historical division: the Mass of the Catechumens[137] first, and then from the Offertory onward, the Mass of the Faithful, from which all but the baptized were excluded. And each of these main parts comprises a twofold movement: there is first the offering to God, and only then the receiving of the gift from God. You have the confession of sins, the prayer for mercy in the *Kyrie*, the song of praise, which is the *Gloria*, and then the *united* prayers for the needs of all. Then, when this duty of offering prayer has been fulfilled, you have the gift from God: the gift of truth in the readings and the Gospel. Similarly with the main part of the Mass: Offertory and Consecration come first, and only then the gift from God, the Supper.

The offering to God is an offering of sorrow, praise, and thanks. But it is an offering *per Christum*, *through* Christ and *with* Christ; and it is an offering made perfect because, through the sacrament, it is made not only with Christ but *in* Christ. *Tu mutaberis in me:* you shall be changed into me.

But if it is made in Christ, then it is also made in the unity of the family whose Head He is. "Pray, brethren," the priest tells us, "that my sacrifice and yours may be acceptable." It is the sacrifice of the whole family, and we are all the offerers; the act of worship is a social act of worship. That is the importance of the renewal of the Church's Liturgy — it is not

[137] The first part of the Mass, up to the Offertory. In the early Church, it was the part of the Mass that catechumens — those preparing for Baptism — were permitted to attend.

primarily an aesthetic but a theological reform. The Mass is not a spectacle at which the faithful are to assist, but an act in which they are to take part. And they take their part, not only with the official priest at the altar, but with their brothers and sisters in the church.

In the primitive days, there was the immediate connection of the Mass with the *Agape*, the love-feast of the faithful;[138] nowadays there is the same thing expressed in symbol in the ceremony of the *pax*, the kiss of peace.

If you bring your gift to the altar and there remember that your brother has anything against you, you must go first and be reconciled. The supper is a family feast.

The Eucharist helps us to see Christ in others

You shall be changed into me: it is the whole family which is thus to be changed, and by being changed to become a unity. The reverence we should feel for all God's creatures and in particular for men and women is here intensified a thousand-fold, for now we have to see Christ Himself in one another. When you see the Blessed Sacrament, you recognize Christ's presence and kneel. When you meet those who have just come from receiving Communion, will you ignore this same presence within them? For they, too, are the bearers of God into the world.

It is good to think of the sins against charity, the sins we are sometimes inclined to regard as of small consequence, in this

[138] The common religious meal in the early Church, closely related to the Eucharist.

light: when we have supped at this same table and gone out again into the world with Infinity in our hearts, how can we so soon forget, and fall into these petty sins which are so grave a betrayal of love and reverence?

The Eucharist unites us to do God's work

It is the *sacrificed* Christ that we receive, and so the sacrament is one of unity in yet a wider sense. We are to be one body, not in any sectarian and exclusive sense. We are to be a unity, not *against* the world, but precisely in order that, in the strength of this common life, we may together be bearers of God into the world, and that learning, through poverty, meekness, and the rest, to let God shine forth from us, we may help to make His redemptive purposes possible in the world.

This is indeed what the common priesthood of the faithful implies. And this is surely why the ending of the Mass, after Communion, is so short compared with the lengthy preparation. With Communion done, there are the brief Communion and post-Communion prayers and then "Go, the Mass is ended." Why? Because this ending is precisely a beginning: you are to go and take up the daily task; to do your work in the world; and to make operative in the world the sacrifice you have just offered and received.[139]

The Mass is the central point in the day: all of the Church's Liturgy centers on it. The Mass gives the official and unofficial

[139] This, of course, does not mean that we should not stay a little after the Mass, to be close in love and worship to Him who has been given to us, and to thank Him for the mercy thus shown us in spite of our sin, and the blessing thus given to the day.

prayer of the family and all the work of the family their value and their redemptive power: Go, then, and begin your work in the strength of that food; go and spread about you in the world the power of love, because now you have Love within you — you abide in Him and He in you.

We must radiate Christ's love

It is part of the integrity of family life, as we shall see, to be outward-turning, to be not an enclosed and aloof community, but a center of life and light for the world outside. And what is true of the human home is true of the greater home which is the Church. "I will draw all things to me," Jesus said;[140] but His will is to make His family, His Church, an invitation in His name.

Sometimes we are not an invitation but an obstacle. Many are seeking Him, and without success: they have heard that He is the God of Love, and they look for His presence among men and fail to find it. Is it always their fault? When you have a family which is obviously a unity forged by love, and a love so strong that it radiates outward and colors the world around it, then you say, "Love lives there" — but is our religious family like that?

This is the failure we should regret most bitterly, and most vigorously determine to remedy: we bear within us the Infinity which can heal the entire world, and instead of acting in that power and blessing the world and bringing it peace, unity, and happiness, we increase the discords and the divisions and

[140] John 12:32.

prolong the travail and the pain. So we turn directly against the purpose of the sacrament. He that eateth my flesh and drinketh my blood abideth in me, and I in him: to live in Christ *must* include as its secondary effect to share Christ's love of creation and so to share in His work for the healing of creation.

The Eucharist restores and renews the world

St. Thomas Aquinas is honored as the Doctor of the Eucharist. It is very fitting; and not only because he wrote of this sacrament itself supremely well. The Eucharist is the greatest restoring power in and for the world: in it all things are made new. It is then the greatest affirmation of the value of created things, of their goodness, for if anything were wholly evil, it could not be restored. And so it is also the great affirmation of the unity of all things in that single act of worship and sacrifice which is the Cross.

But it is just this which is the essence of St. Thomas's teaching. When he writes of marriage, be speaks of Manicheism,[141] with his usual exactitude, as *pessima haeresis*, the worst of heresies: you cannot say that matter is evil for this, too, comes from God and, where man is concerned, is an essential part of worship.

Nor, for St. Thomas, can there be that opposition between this world and the next, between nature and grace, which you find in some Christian thinkers. The divine life works in and

[141] The heresy of dualism that teaches that a cosmic conflict exists between a good realm of light and an evil realm of darkness, and that matter belongs to the evil realm.

through nature; engraced nature has to serve and worship God, and labor to remedy as far as possible the effects of the original turning away.

St. Thomas is the Doctor of the Eucharist, then, because he is the expounder of this great affirmation: all things are good in themselves, although evil has damaged and twisted them; all things are renewed and blessed by the presence of the sacrificed Christ in the world, by the power of Christ made operative through the souls and bodies of His faithful, who share His life and His love. But the corollary of this affirmation, the affirmation of the liberty of the glory of the sons of God, is the giving of thanks. That is what the word *eucharist* means, and in this, too, therefore the title is justified.

"To them that love God, all things work together unto good":[142] this expresses that loving sense of the ceaseless Providence of God, the sense that what is, is His will and therefore must work unto good, and that all our efforts are part of that all-inclusive love and care so that we, for our part, are free, carefree, if only we do at each present moment the best we can. All this conviction, together with the deep happiness it produces, is in our belief in the Eucharist, and therefore is an essential part of our worship when we worship, as we must, through the Eucharist.

"I draw all things to myself"; and "behold I make all things new":[143] that is the summary of the doctrine of the Eucharist; and to say that we must share in this double movement is to summarize our part in the doctrine of the Eucharist. If ever it

[142] Rom. 8:28.

[143] Rev. 21:5.

could be said of us that all our words were enlightenment, solace, and strength, our touch always healing, our eyes wise and gentle, and our whole life an epiphany of the power of love, then it would mean that we had been fully faithful at last to the greatest of all the sacraments. Men would be able to say of us, as of Him in whom we live, "We have seen their glory; and of their fullness we have all received."[144]

[144] Cf. John 1:14, 16.

Chapter Seven

Blessed are the merciful, for they shall obtain mercy.

Matt. 5:7

Mercy

In this beatitude, we are given a yet more emphatic repudiation of the policy of the ivory tower. We are all involved in the life of the family, and all responsible for it. As we have seen, we have a duty toward it in justice, but justice is not enough. And indeed, once you accept the idea that the race of man is God's family and yours, the fact that justice is not enough becomes obvious: who could imagine a happy family life based exclusively on justice?

St. Thomas remarks that "some withdraw themselves from works of mercy *lest* they be involved in other people's misery." Most of us would have to plead guilty to doing this at some time or another — "I simply cannot go and see that poor old woman; it makes me miserable for the rest of the day" — but it is clearly the denial of the whole substance of family life. And our Lord is quite definite: it is not by doing this that we shall find happiness, but by doing exactly the contrary, by being merciful.

Why?

The first reason has already been stated: only by being merciful can you live in the family, and only by living the life of the family can you be fully alive. But there is a second reason. St. Thomas has a further remark which, at first, may seem somewhat arbitrary: this beatitude, he says, is connected with the gift of counsel, which concerns the choice of means to attain the desired end, and which, therefore, particularly concerns "those things which are *most* useful to the end, namely, mercy."[145]

Mercy is generous

And why is mercy thus singled out above all other good qualities? Surely because it is the greatest possible repudiation of the kingdom of mammon, the farthest from the selfish struggle for *my* rights, *my* pleasure, *my* comfort, and *my* privacy. Mercy is in those who have already learned to think and to will in terms of the family.

Justice is not enough. You have here a virtue which goes beyond the demands of justice: the virtue of generosity, which leads us, says St. Thomas, to give freely to friends and others who are specially united to us, and with whom, therefore, we do not think in terms of mere justice.

Poverty and detachment make us openhanded. Meekness and the ability to choose discomfort make us further forgetful of ourselves. Fortitude gives us the large-heartedness which can be magnificent in its giving. And the love which is the stuff of real friendship — as of family life — makes us long to give lavishly, for in love, giving is itself the highest form of receiving.

[145] Cf. *Summa Theologica*, II-II, Q. 52, art. 4.

Compassion focuses on the needs of others

Beyond the virtue there is the gift.[146] We are right to have a special place in our hearts for our own family and friends, but if we are to live as Christians, then the whole world has to be our family, and all men our friends. The gift goes farther because it considers one thing only: the *need* of others.

In the last chapter, we were thinking of the Lord's Supper; now we are in the context of the parable of the supper: "Go out into the highways and hedges and *compel* them to come in, that my table may be filled."[147] The gift considers only the need of the outcasts, the publicans and sinners, and the waifs and strays, and because of their need, must give them a special love and reverence.

Let us underline this word *reverence* in our minds: unless we have this, we may have compassion indeed, but not the compassion which is the gift of the Spirit. For this compassion you learn by learning to be reverent and docile toward God; it is a gift you *receive*. And when you hold it out in your hands to another, you must remember whence it came; you must remember that only in abasement of spirit can you pass on a gift which is divine; and you must remember and imitate the

[146] St. Thomas, as we have just seen, links this beatitude with the gift of counsel; elsewhere he connects it with the gift of piety. Here, for the sake of brevity, I speak simply of the "gift of pity," meaning by that the impulse of the Spirit through these gifts in teaching, inspiring, and directing the soul in the way of the merciful. [Because of the negative connotation of the word *pity* in modern usage, *compassion*, which more accurately captures the author's meaning, has been used in place of *pity* throughout these pages. — ED.]

[147] Luke 14:23.

compassion of Mary the sinner when she anointed the feet of Christ, a compassion which was divine precisely because in one action she expressed her own abasement and sorrow, and her compassion for the wayworn feet of God.

The gift of compassion leads us to perfection

We are here at the very center of the way of perfection. If you would be perfect, go, sell all you have, and give to the poor:[148] in the literal sense, it is the poverty of the vows and the cloister; but its spirit is not to be confined to the cloister, for its spirit is simply the ideal of charity. Be ready to give anything you have when your brother is in need; be ready to sacrifice your possessions, your comfort, your time, and all that you have, not only for the sake of those who are dearest to you, but for the sake of any outcasts: compel them to come in, compel them with the power of love, that the table may be filled — and what a glory it is to bring the suffering and the needy to God's table.

We are at the center of the way of perfection because we are exactly at that point where the Faith becomes not something acknowledged with the mind, but something burning and shining through the heart that all may see. We are at the point where the love of God does, in truth, become that visible demonstration of the gospel for which the world is waiting and looking. "See how these Christians love one another!"[149] People have heard it said so often in derision

[148] Matt. 19:21.

[149] Tertullian, *Apology*, ch. 39, sect. 7.

down the ages of history; they miss the innumerable humble lives in which it has been a blazing truth, and see only the scandals of the sects, schisms, wars, and hatreds which have stained and rent the seamless robe of Christ.[150]

But live this beatitude, learn to make your whole life an expression and fulfillment, a channel, of the divine compassion, and they will forget all they have heard and all they have learned from their history books, because they will be able to look into your heart and see His glory, the glory of the only-begotten of the Father, full of grace and truth.

We must avoid individualism and materialism

Why is it, people ask, that Christians are no better than non-Christians, if all that they claim for their Faith is true? And the answer, insofar as the accusation is true, must be that we are influenced far more deeply than we know by the individualism we inherit and the selfish materialism with which we are surrounded.

We are busy with the defense of man's right to property, and so we must be; but only if we remember that we are advocating no absolute right, only if we take care that, in opposing one error, we do not fall into a worse one. We have a right to property, yes; but every right implies a corresponding duty. The right to property implies a duty to the common good, and the more we have, the greater our responsibility for that common good. We have a right to property, but only within the life of charity. We have a right to a home; but it must be not a fortress

[150] John 19:23.

from which all are excluded, but a home where all can find a welcome.

The gift of compassion enables us to be lavish

As with material possessions of every sort, so with all that we have and are, the gift enables us to be humbly and royally lavish, and above all with the gift of compassion itself. You must be lavish, first of all, to those nearest to you, those you love most; but you must also be lavish to those who are most in need; you must be lavish to your enemies — or rather to those who think themselves your enemies, for it takes two to make an enemy.

You must have compassion for all, and the greatest compassion for those who have the greatest need of it. But you must do so humbly, reverently, not conferring a gift, but asking to be given one; otherwise you will have not compassion but the terrifying vulgarity of condescension and all the ugliness of pride. (Think for a moment of whether you are ever shocked: if you are, it is a lack of wisdom, for you ought to know more about human nature, including your own; it is a lack of humility, for you are presupposing that the thing that shocks you is something far below your own moral level — and if that is the way you think, then you will never have the gift of divine compassion.)

We must have compassion for all persons

We have been thinking much of the life of the family. Think of this gift of compassion in terms of family life; it is easy, then, to apply it to the larger family of the world. Think first of the perhaps unconscious, perhaps hotly repudiated, need of the young for compassion from the old, and of how easy it is to forget that need and so to be destructive: you forget or you deride and lacerate the keen sensitiveness, the soaring hopes, the innocence that goes with the lack of hard, and hardening, experience. If you have compassion for these things, you can strengthen and upbuild, and where necessary, you can heal and restore; without compassion you may easily turn growing experience into poison and despair.

Think, on the other hand, of the need of the old for compassion from the young. Remember the pathos of the divine words to Peter: "But when thou art old another shall gird thee, and shall lead thee whither thou wouldst not."[151] Remember the long pain of dwindling strength and power, the loneliness of those whose friends have left them behind, the sorrow of happier memories, and the feeling of becoming a stranger as the younger generations establish their new and strange ways. Remember that the slownesses, the disabilities of mind and body, and the oddities of behavior which most arouse the impatience of the young are themselves a cross and perhaps the result of many earlier crosses. If you have compassion for these things, you can give strength as well as solace, and perhaps you can turn a Purgatory into a joy; but if you lack compassion, you may well bring bitterness into the last days of a human life — and how shall you efface *that* stain?

Remember the Mass, to which all creation is brought so that it may be redeemed and blessed. We must not think of

[151] John 21:18.

bringing only the lovely things and the noble things and the things of good report: we are to bring the sorrows and uglinesses of the world that they may be cleansed; we are to bring the heart of man that it may be purified and made gentle, and compassionate toward human sin and human stupidity, as Christ was compassionate.

For when you remember the Mass, remember the Cross. Remember what the eyes of Christ beheld from the height of the Cross — not only the immediate unimaginable crime and the malice of those who watched and jeered, but all the sin in all the hearts of men then living, and then, backward through the ages, all the sin from the beginning, and onward into future ages to the end of time, even though now the Light was in the world. Remember all the weight of all the evil of all creation, and then remember that He prayed for them because they were ignorant.

God's compassion is always present in our lives

Remember the tears Christ shed in compassion over Jerusalem, but do not think that this is something which is faded into the past; do not think that although God could weep over Jerusalem, He cannot weep now over the sorrows of earthly cities. The tears were shed at a moment in time, yes; but God is not in time, and the sorrow and compassion of God are present with us, with every cry and every tear drawn from men's bewildered — or perhaps hardened and blasphemous — hearts. The eyes of Christ wept, and now can weep no more, but the actions of Christ are the actions of God in whom is no change, no past, no history, but the single moment of the eternal present. And because of the Incarnation of the Word, there is unchangeably in the heart of that eternal present the mystery of the compassion and sorrow of God.

God's compassion is redemptive

But we must understand compassion aright, as we must understand comfort aright. The compassion of Christ, which is this gift of the Spirit, is a *redemptive* compassion that heals, strengthens, and upbuilds — the compassion that said to the poor woman, "Go, and now sin no more." That is why those who have it are so immeasurably far from the withering pride of condescension: the quality of this mercy is not strained[152] (for it has the freedom from all narrowness, all bounds, and all reserves and inhibiting prejudices, of the wind that bloweth where it listeth[153]); it droppeth as the gentle rain from heaven,[154] the rain that makes the earth fertile, renews it, and causes it to bring forth again its fruit; it is the healing touch that raises men, restores them to wholeness, and gives them the courage to start again.

Our sense of compassion increases with our sense of sin

Perhaps this is what you must have the most compassion for, as Christ seems to have had: the sin of the world that comes of stupidity. You must never, of course, for an instant let

[152] Cf. William Shakespeare, *The Merchant of Venice*, Act 4, scene 1.
[153] John 3:8.
[154] Cf. Deut. 32:2.

your compassion be degraded into sentimentality, so that you cease to regard sin as important or culpable, or brush away with a gesture the real evils, the pride, malice, and cruelty that tear the world. But there is so much wrongdoing that springs from ignorance. "They know not what they do":[155] they are deluded, or their judgments are mistaken. Sometimes the sins against Christ and His Church can be an attempt to *serve* Christ and His Church.

And then there are all the sins of human frailty: the flesh lusteth against the spirit, and we do those things we would not do;[156] and for these, too, in others, you must have compassion. The quality of mercy is not strained.

"He that hath the substance of this world and shall see his brother in need and shall shut up his bowels from him: how doth the charity of God abide in him?"[157] Perhaps you have the substance of eternal life, the gift of faith, which is yours through no merit of your own. If you see your brother in need of this, and shut up your bowels from him, how shall the charity of God abide in you?

Think, in this connection, once again of the petty sins: the censoriousness, the scandalmongering, the touchiness and ill temper, and the desire to show people up, to prove your own superiority. Think of all the small nagging ways in which the life of the family can be withered and made parched and arid, and compare it with this gentle rain from heaven. Then the sense of sin will grow in you, and with it the sense of

[155] Luke 23:34.
[156] Gal. 5:17.
[157] 1 John 3:17.

compassion, for the two go together. "Forgive us our trespasses as we forgive those who trespass against us": if you have compassion for others, you will obtain mercy yourself; but equally if you know in the depths of your soul your own need of mercy, you will have compassion for your brother.

And your compassion will be the divine compassion because your offering of it will itself be the asking of a favor. "Behold, I stand at the gate and knock":[158] omnipotence becomes a mendicant because it is part of the nature of love that it must ask to be allowed to give.

La colère des imbéciles remplit le monde — the world is filled, and racked and torn, by the fury of fools, and the base things are exalted and the lovely things destroyed; but still you must have compassion.

Compassion is woman's special vocation

If you are a woman, then remember that this is your special vocation, the vocation of women; and until you have fulfilled that vocation, you will never be made whole.

The male mind, the rational mind, has its schemes and ambitions. It tries to order the economy of the world, to marshal events, dictate policies, and build up the outward structure of life. It has great pride, the pride of the creator, in its achievements, and it likes to think that it is self-sufficient, and that it battles with destiny and orders chaos alone and unaided. But reason without intuition, the male without the female mind, is often blind and often stupid. And one day its

[158] Rev. 3:20.

house of cards falls around it, the long labor and the mighty ambitions are turned to dust, and then there is emptiness.

And then it is time for women to fulfill their vocation; to have compassion on the rational stupidity of men. The gentle rain has to fall on the withered soil of the soul of the man, and renew it; you have to have compassion in order to heal and restore and re-create. Then, in your compassion, you yourself are made whole. You will not be made whole until then, until you have let this fumbling arrogance grope its way to your different and deeper wisdom and from the womb of your compassion be born again.

"Son, behold thy mother":[159] you have in Mary the Mother of Mercy the figure of what you have to be. It may be particular men — husband, children, friends — who will come to you so; it may be your vocation to share with Mary something of her universal compassion, but to renew the soil of the world only indirectly, through your own inner experience and your unexpressed compassion. But somehow, in some way, you must share her vocation, you must share the glory of the destiny of which she is the symbol and the supreme expression. For only so can you share as you should in the restoring of the world, and only so will you yourself be made whole.

The gift of compassion makes us whole

Compassion is the special vocation of women, but of course it is not confined to women. Others too have special need of it: those whose gift is to have in a marked degree the qualities

[159] John 19:27.

of mind of both man and woman, to be rational and intuitive, such as the artists and men of genius; those whose special office requires this two-sided quality of mind, such as the priest, who is representative of *Mother* Church, and the doctors and surgeons whose special vocation is to heal; and those who have care of the frailness of childhood. These need the gift of compassion if they, in their turn, are to be made whole through their special destinies to serve the world.

But we all must have the substance of the gift of compassion if we are to obtain compassion; and all of us will, in fact, have it if we have learned to be humble and to mourn.

For compassion is indeed the corollary of humility and repentance: you can no longer, if you have learned the sense of sin, speak of your brother with arrogance as a sinner. We are each responsible for all. You will not say, when you see some evil done, "There but for the grace of God go I"; you will say, "There go I." You will not say, "How these are hurting the heart of Christ," but "How I, in these, am hurting the heart of Christ." For you will know yourself implicated and responsible. And there will be shame and sorrow in your compassion because you have not done more to avert the evil and have not perhaps even prayed for these who are the immediate cause of the evil.

But you will hardly think in terms of praying for sinners: you will think of praying for others, and especially of praying for your sin in others. These, you will say, have gone astray and perhaps they are at war with the Good, but why has not power gone forth from me to help heal them, as it went forth from Him who has sent me to be a bearer of His power? These are searching for God, and they are miserable because they cannot find Him — and have I even prayed that they may find Him?

Sentimentality and self-pity destroy the power of compassion

Let us repeat: we must never for an instant allow compassion to degenerate into sentimentality. We must be as hard as iron in our estimate of the gravity and horror of sin; we must never minimize anything, nor excuse anything by explaining it away. Compassion essentially depends on clarity of vision: you become most fully merciful when you become clean of heart. But you must be able to see the two things with equal clarity: the nature of sin in itself, the immaturity in evil of the human heart.

There is something more. You will degrade your compassion, perhaps you will destroy altogether the power of compassion in you, if you pity yourself. If there is one thing more humiliating than to say, "How good I am," it is to say, "How unfortunate and ill-treated I am." The essential condition of this gift of divine compassion for others is to be convinced, not of your need of compassion for your sad fate, but of your need of mercy for your sins. If you are the victim of self-pity, you may feel sad and sympathetic for others, although it is hardly likely perhaps; but your compassion will certainly stop short at the softness of solace: it will be unable to strengthen and upbuild. And that is the whole purpose of the divine compassion. If, on the other hand, you know your own need of mercy, then your eyes will be turned on God; you will be able to be the instrument of His own gift of compassion, and so you will give new heart to others; you will not only console, but strengthen and sustain.

Compassion increases our capacity for joy

Happy are the merciful, for they shall obtain mercy. To obtain mercy, says St. Thomas, is more even than to have one's fill, because it means that man receives more than he merited or *was even able to desire*. If we have the sense of sin, we want God's mercy, and to receive that is much indeed. But we need His mercy more than we want it, for we need it more than we can know.

But there is more even than that. The merciful shall obtain more even than they can desire. And how is that? Because compassion enlarges the heart, and where there is infinite compassion, there is an infinite enlargement of the heart, and so an infinite capacity for joy — and what the joy is, no man can tell.

The pain of the world and the gift of counsel

Amen, amen I say to you, unless the grain of wheat falling into the ground die, itself remaineth alone. But if it die, it bringeth forth much fruit. . . . If any man minister to me, let him follow me: and where I am, there also shall my minister be.[160]

The gift of counsel is concerned with the choice of means to the desired end. You must make your whole life a single God-ward movement, so that everything you do and have and are becomes functional, becomes part of that movement. Therefore you have to see all that happens in the light of the unity of God's Providence.

For all this you need the gift of counsel, and you need it especially where it is especially hard to see God's love and Providence: in the problem of pain.[161]

There are two extreme positions here, and both of them are unchristian.

[160] John 12:24-26.

[161] We have already mentioned in chapter five the Christian doctrine of the threefold value of suffering for the Christian himself. Here we are concerned not with this but simply with the attempt to find, for the onlooker, some explanation of the problem of pain.

Pain is neither to be avoided at all costs nor glorified as a good

There is first the quest of invulnerability: the determination to avoid pain at all costs, as being the greatest of all evils. This attitude is unchristian because it refuses to see that pain can often have a positive value: not only as an ascetic training of character, but also as a means to a deeper awareness and understanding.

On the other hand, there is the glorification of pain as something good in itself, an end rather than a means, so that all attempts to alleviate it — by increased medical skill, for example — are regarded as immoral. This attitude is unchristian too, for it forgets, or at least minimizes, the redemptive presence of Christ in the world. There is sin and therefore there is suffering, but the life and the power are with us to overcome the sin and in some degree to alleviate, or transform, the suffering, as the Church does by prayer and the laying on of hands. Pain is an effect of evil; it can also be a means to good; if you make it not a means but an end, you deny the nature of God, and blaspheme.

The Christian position, then, is neither of these extremes. It accepts pain, directly as the effect of evil in the world, indirectly as a gift from God, because out of evil good may come. It acknowledges the duty of redeeming the world from pain in the end; but it acknowledges the duty of redeeming the world *through* pain, as a means. Pain has its redemptive purpose; but sometimes it is hard to see this, and often it is hard to accept the fact and act accordingly. So we need the gift of counsel.

Counsel helps us to understand pain correctly

We need the gift of counsel to see clearly ourselves, and still more to be able to help others to see. If you misunderstand and misinterpret the Christian attitude, you can do great harm: if you turn it into something morbid, if you treat pain as good in itself, you turn the religion of love into a grey cult that kills the joy in life and makes a travesty of the goodness of God. And the misinterpretation leads, in practice, to disaster: the Church has always taught man's need of gaiety and joy, and if you deny this wisdom, you destroy the health of the spirit and end in neurosis or in death of soul.

Suffering is a means to an end, and therefore there is a reason for it. It is part of the plot of a love-story, and we must see it as such.

God permits suffering for our good

Does God rejoice in suffering? There has to be a double answer. In itself, no, of course not; good cannot rejoice in evil as such. As a means from which good will come, yes, if by *rejoicing* we mean willing the end which includes the indirect willing of the means, and is accompanied by compassion.

Only thus indirectly is suffering caused by God: the good His love wills for us may have the effect of hurting us here and now; but the hurt is not what He directly wills, and that it *is* a hurt for us is the result of our sin. In giving man the gift of freedom, He gives him the freedom to sin, and from sin, the evil of suffering follows; but also by suffering, the sin can be expiated and its effects in some measure remedied.

The pain of the world is not the final thing, as sin itself is not the final thing. The Word was made flesh, and dwells among us; the power to restore the world is in the world. The revelation of the glory is given to us if we have eyes to see, and it is compatible with goodness and compassion to rejoice in the fact of suffering if the suffering is what causes us to see.

That is exactly what suffering can, in fact, do, and why it is part of the plot of the love-story. Sin and, therefore, suffering are permitted by the eternal Providence because after sin is the Cross, and in the Cross is the revelation of the depths of love, the mercy and the compassion of God. You need suffering of one sort or another to become adult in love; you need it to understand the depths of love and the depths of compassion because you need it in order to *experience* the deepest truths and realities.

But does that explain the sufferings of children, and of the animals? Does it explain, not the ready acceptance of necessary suffering, but the desire for suffering which is not inevitable, on the part of the saints? No, there is something more.

Suffering that seems senseless can be redemptive

The saint *must* share Christ's suffering, as we have seen. It is the nature of love. But also we are a family: we are each responsible for all. Your suffering is meant to be redemptive, not for yourself merely, but for the world. The pain of Christ is redemptive for all humanity, to bring to all humanity the gifts of understanding, love, and sorrow. You can share in that universality by your own pain, and if you love Christ enough, you will be impelled to share.

There are mysteries of substitution that we cannot fathom, but which the saints have sensed: their choice of avoidable pain is not an assertion that pain is an end in itself, but, among other things, a living proof that we are a family.

But what about children and animals?

You must go deeper still. These things are in themselves part of that chain of cause and effect which the primal evil set in motion in the world. But although we are all involved because we are all responsible for evil, and therefore must avert or diminish the pain where we can, that is not all. We are a family even when we remain unconscious of our oneness: wherever pain is, the deeper realities can be revealed to the world. The child or the animal in pain can in this way share in Christ's redemptive compassion.

But do they themselves have nothing from it? Do they remain simply the innocent victims of the evil of the world, and have no recompense?

On the contrary, the Providence of God is not made ineffective by the creature's unawareness of it: you can begin to work out your salvation from evil, you can be led by God toward His mercy and your own restoration, even though you are unaware of what is being done in you. "He that is mighty hath done great things in me":[162] perhaps there is an echo of this receiving of an unlooked-for glory in the effect of uncomprehended suffering. We do not know what glory springs for the child in eternity from his puzzled pain on earth. And may not God also, in His mercy, be fashioning the child's soul secretly to depths of love and understanding which he would

162 Luke 1:49.

otherwise miss? His power to mold us is not limited to an appeal to the conscious mind.

Even animals' suffering can have a restoring effect

But the animal has no immortal soul. Nonetheless, there are three things perhaps which we can say. First, we must not be sentimental: we must not pretend to ourselves that animals have the same consciousness, and therefore the same capacity for suffering, as man. That does not do away with the problem, but it lessens it.

Secondly, sympathy, the desire to co-suffer, seems to be found in some of the animals which man has "reclaimed." It is the function of the animal creation to minister to man; and to fulfill a proper function, even though it is not fully recognized as such, is to have some sense of fulfillment, or at least to have comfort in pain. And now that the animal creation must minister not only by serving man through its labor but by leading him to understanding through its pain, perhaps we can sometimes dimly discern some possibility of compensation in the midst of the pain.

But thirdly, you find that the more primitive peoples are, the less they have of individual consciousness and the more consciousness of the group, the herd; and if this is to be verified still more of the animals, then perhaps you can see the restoring function of uncomprehended suffering in this light. For the mind to find any peace in the thought of the suffering of the child, you must be able to see how the child itself has his sorrow turned into joy. But if anywhere there is only the herd-consciousness, then perhaps you have some comfort and explanation in the idea (and is it impossible that animals should have some sort of instinctive awareness of it?) that the pain will bring its benefit to the herd. It will bring its benefit because it is part of that Providence which is not made ineffective because of a lack of conscious apprehension of it, that Providence which will in the end bring out of all this germination of (even unconscious) redemptive suffering the flowering of a new and more radiant earth.

Counsel helps us understand and bear suffering

With great labor of the mind we can perhaps dimly discern some sort of partial explanation of the harder aspects of the problem of pain. But consider how much we need the gift of the Spirit to convince the mind and bring it peace; how much we need the gift if we are to *know* that "all things work together unto good."

We need the gift also to enable us to live by this knowledge. Suffering can be, and is meant to be, a means to strength and to depth and clarity of vision. It is meant to be a means to love. It is meant to safeguard us against superficiality, against finding a refuge from God in the externals of religion. It is meant to show us sin as a cosmic thing, for which we share the responsibility; and therefore it is meant to lead us to the love that longs to atone and restore.

We need the gift for all this: to show us what is best to be done, how best we are to carry out God's Providence. We need the strength of the gift to accept or to choose things that are costly, and to make them an expression of love and a sharing in the redemptive sufferings of Christ. We need the gift to turn the pain that comes to us or the pain we choose into creative joy. And we need the gift, finally, to ensure that pain shall lead us, not into self-pity or complacency, not into a concentration on our own selves, but into a greater love and service of the family.

Our suffering enables us to offer compassion and comfort to others

The gift of counsel is especially concerned with mercy. We shall use suffering aright if we use it to increase our compassion; and we shall use it to increase our compassion most fully if we use it — or rather allow the Spirit to use it in us — to increase our power to give counsel to others.

The Mother of Mercy is also the Mother of Good Counsel: we must imitate her in the one as in the other. When you have learned understanding and wisdom and the meaning of the divine compassion from God's gift of pain, then you can pass on the wisdom and the good counsel to others, and that wisdom and good counsel will be the fine flower of compassion. You will be able to minister to Christ because you will be able to speak with the voice of Christ, and so to bring to others His comfort and strength.

Unless the grain of wheat die, itself remaineth alone. You must learn through the pain of the world to be born again in the new life; but the new life is a fruitful life — fruitful for the whole world, because it ministers to Christ, it acts in and for Christ, and it expresses the wisdom and compassion of the Cross. To be a man or woman of good counsel, you must learn the Christian attitude toward suffering. There is something lacking even to the most brilliant mind until it has deep experience of love, and the way to that is suffering. For out of the wisdom begotten of suffering, peace is born; and it is when you have peace in the depths of your soul that you can give good counsel.

The prayer of sorrow helps us in three ways

We were thinking, in an earlier chapter, of the prayer of piety, which goes beyond the prayer of awe because it includes the trusting familiarity of the child. Now we should think a little of the prayer of sorrow — the expression of the sense of sin and of our responsibility for the pain of the world.

God is terrible. We need the prayer of sorrow to keep familiarity and reverent and full of holy fear. We need it, in any case, because it is a necessary part of repentance and humility. We need it also because it is part of our redemptive compassion: it is a necessary part of that acceptance of pain which restores the world.

Our contrition must be a creative redeeming of the past

We must first pray our sorrow for our own sins. Here it is important to remember that contrition is not an uncreative remorse, a brooding over the past; rather, it is a creative redeeming of the past, because these sins are an evil out of which good — the good of greater understanding and love — can come, and the sorrow is what thus turns them to good and so creates the future. And this creative purpose of the prayer of sorrow should determine it in practice. Normally it is unwise and wasteful to go over the past in detail, and we should think rather of our general sinfulness or of the main ways in which sinfulness has been expressed in us. Only when a clearer vision shows us more adequately an evil that hitherto we had treated lightly should we, normally speaking, make it the special material of our thought and prayer, so that it, too, may be turned more completely, by being more completely repented of, to future good.

Then we must pray our sorrow for all the sin of the world, because of our share of responsibility for it. We should pray our sorrow for the Original Sin as well, for in this, too, we are all implicated. The essence of all the evil in the universe is the attempt of the creature to repudiate its dependence and become a god. The only way in which the evil can be overcome and turned into good is by reversing this movement and reasserting our creatureliness, and this we can only do by repentance and sorrow.

The prayer of sorrow becomes the prayer of compassion

It is first and foremost the sin as such, the offense against God, that we must be sorry for. But we must not forget the suffering it causes, and here the prayer of sorrow turns into the prayer of compassion: "They have no wine."

The beauty of the world is ravaged, the purity sullied, the joy quenched, and the harmony destroyed: it is in part my fault, and at least I must pray my sorrow, that to some extent I may undo the evil, and the earth to some extent may be restored. We can never return to the earthly paradise; there are some things that can never be changed, however long the world goes on. But at least I can take the pain I am given or the pain I choose and turn them into loving sorrow and into the prayer of sorrow, and so increase a little the renewed sanctification and blessing, and the joy, of the world.

"If any man minister to me, let him follow me; and where I am, there also shall my minister be." If we are to administer the divine compassion through our sorrow, we must follow: and where will He be? He will be wherever there is need of compassion and good counsel, in the dark places of the world, wherever there is squalor, suffering, stupidity, and sin.

And how shall we be able to follow? We shall follow only if we are, like Him, men of sorrow and acquainted with infirmity,[163] filled with the sense of our own sin as He was filled with the sense of the sin of all the world. But if we use our power to follow Him wherever He goes, then, administering His mercy, we shall ourselves obtain mercy; giving good counsel, we shall ourselves be made wise; healing others, we shall ourselves be healed. Our sorrow will bring mercy and joy to our own selves, but to the self in the greatest and widest sense of the word: to the self as living in union with the whole universe of which it is a part. We shall know the redemptive power of compassion because, in the renewal of the soul by Christ, we shall know ourselves to be a part of that universal process whereby the omnipotent compassion makes all things new.

[163] Cf. Isa. 53:3.

C. The Sacrament of this Beatitude

Anointing of the Sick

"Amen, amen I say to thee, when thou wast younger, thou didst gird thyself and didst walk where thou wouldst. But when thou shalt be old, thou shalt stretch forth thy hands and another shall gird thee and lead thee whither thou wouldst not." And when He had said this, He saith to him, "Follow me."[164]

The account of the Church's custody of the energy of good in the world, its divine power to heal, sanctify, and bless, is not complete until we have thought of this sacrament of the Anointing of the Sick. Its purpose is to strengthen us in the last great crisis, the last great turning point, of life. And we think of it as the sacrament of old age, when strength and vitality are at their lowest ebb, and death and the unknown life are very near. But we cannot be too strong or too full of vitality to learn a lesson from the theology of the sacrament.

We are told that it has a fourfold purpose. It frees the mind from the trouble and fright that attend the thought of the coming of death; it heals the body if a renewal of health is for our good; it purifies the soul of sin; and it takes away, to greater or lesser extent, the weakness of soul and the need of

[164] John 21:18, 19.

punishment, of purgation, which sin has caused. So it is described as *consummatium totius vitae christianae*, as what brings the whole Christian life to a completion, because if health is, in fact, not to be restored, this sacrament immediately disposes us for the "entry into glory."[165]

Death is the last and greatest crisis, but it should be a completion of something, not a termination; it should be a stage in the total story, a beginning rather than an end. The *Ite, missa est*[166] at Mass is less an end than a beginning: you have received the life and the power, and now you must go forth into the world and begin the redemptive work of the day. In the same way, the coming of death to the Christian should be an *Ite, missa est:* you have received the life and the power, and the constant mercy of God throughout your life has brought you slowly nearer and nearer to complete possession by, and oneness with, the indwelling Trinity. Now in the Anointing of the Sick, the process is consummated, and so you are ready to go forth and begin the *vita nuova*, the radiant life of the eternal day.

The saints show us the proper attitude toward death

That is why the death of holy people is a cause for rejoicing, even though we are sad because they are gone from us. If we lived as the saints live, we should meet death as they meet it, with a smile of welcome and joy — because they know that what awaits them is the completion of life, the consummation

[165] Cf. Luke 24:26.

[166] "Go, you are dismissed."

of all happiness, the fulfillment of all desire, and the mercy that gives more even than they are able to desire: the glory of the infinite life and beatitude of the One.

We who are not holy can still learn something of the spirit of the saints. When we face our death, we shall be sad because of the littleness of our faith and frightened because of the greatness of our sin, but there is the sacrament to console and strengthen us.

Remember the symbolism: the body is anointed with oil for strength as for a journey (and so the vague intuition, and the longing, in the rites of the ancient religions are fulfilled), for the body is not done with; there is the resurrection to follow in the fullness of time. We go to a new life, but not as a man going to a new city who must leave behind him all that he loved in the old; we go to the abidingness of the eternal present in which the Beauty we all too dimly loved and desired on earth is to take us forever to Himself. And if we cannot have the perfect joy of the saints, we can still have something of their trust, if we have tried our best to live in love. "They shall obtain mercy": we shall know our need of it then, but if we have tried, we shall not need to be frightened.

Anointing of the Sick helps us prepare for death now

It is good for us to think of this sacrament now, when perhaps death seems very remote from us. We shall be sad at that time because of the lost opportunities of serving God, the failures in responding to His life and power, the lack of understanding of His ways and His purposes, and the sinking back into the rut of mediocre routine. We shall be sad, too, because of our failure to accept with joy the pain and drudgery of life that might have served the family and been turned into the gold of love. We shall be sad, above all, if we have failed to administer the divine compassion and mercy, for then we shall realize, as never before, our own need.

It is good to think of this sacrament now because it can help us now. The effect of this sacrament, we are told, depends on the disposition of him who receives it; but our disposition then will be determined by our life here and now. And one of the things we should remember in this connection is that, although final perseverance is a gift, we can do something to prepare ourselves in the hope of receiving it.

It is not too difficult to love God for a day or a week or a year; but we have to prepare precisely for the *diuturnitas* of the good life — for the difficulty of going on day by day until the end. You remember how Peter, immediately after those words of our Lord which told him of the death he should die, "turning about, saw that disciple whom Jesus loved," and he said, "Lord, and what shall this man do?" And "Jesus saith to him, 'So I shall have him to remain till I come, what is it to thee? Follow thou me.' "[167] For the one, death is soon to come; for the other, there is the long wait — and how agonizingly long for this "disciple whom Jesus loved."

To think of this last crisis in life is to remind ourselves that we have to be prepared for two things, for "You know not when the lord of the house cometh, at evening or at midnight or at the cock-crowing or in the morning":[168] we have to be prepared

[167] John 21:20, 21-22.
[168] Mark 13:35.

to meet death soon and suddenly, and we have to be prepared to work on and on, until evening or midnight.

Abandonment and patience prepare us for death

The first thing, then, is to put ourselves into the hands of Providence, to fashion our wills into identity with the will of the Lord of the house, and accept whatever length of life He may have ordained for us. Then we must set ourselves to be in readiness. That must mean, primarily, to learn to live always in the eternal present.

But it means, also, a training in patience and perseverance. We must not, of course, confuse dryness with death of soul: it is not whether we always feel joy in serving that matters, but whether we always serve.

But there is the danger that sooner or later we may find the will growing tired and relaxing its efforts and so slipping into that lukewarmness of which we were thinking before. The heart that has turned to God may turn away again if its love grows cool. It may be distracted by the pleasant things of life because it isolates them from its worship of God and tries to enjoy them for themselves alone. It may fall into self-deception, and find an interest in godly things but not for the love of God, as a man's purely aesthetic interest in the Liturgy, let us say, may appear to him as a service of God although in fact it is an escape from Him. It may take refuge from the thought of God in ceaseless activity, even though it be a beneficent and religious activity.

There are times when we need a will of iron, not to save us from a conscious turning away from God and the things of

God, but to save us from unconsciously trying to lose our sense of God in a whirl of what would otherwise be praiseworthy activity.

"Another shall gird thee." We need patience to meet the special trials, the weakness and powerlessness of old age; but we need patience also to meet the similar trials that may come upon us at any age: the sorrow of seeing our labors destroyed and being unable to prevent it; the sorrow of seeing our labors fruitless and our dreams unfulfilled; the hardness of having to watch others reap what we have sown; the hardness of having to realize that we have tried for so many years to be good Christians and yet have made so little observable progress.

All these things can give us a sense of powerlessness and therefore of impatience and perhaps a sort of despair. Then we have to draw ourselves back to the thought of the eternal present, the thought of the loving Providence of the divine Wisdom which disposes all things sweetly. We have to try to teach ourselves all over again to care and not to care, to learn to prepare for the future by making what use we can of each moment as it comes, and leaving the rest, without worry, to the mercy of God.

"If any man minister to me, let him follow me."[169] To learn to follow our Lord in His journey of mercy through the world is to learn to live with Him; and to learn to live with Him is to be ready to die. It is to be steeped in the thought of His compassion, and that is a thought which drives out fear.

You find, indeed, in the Gospels that these two themes are constantly recurring: to follow Christ, and to be without fear.

[169] Cf. Matt. 16:24; Mark 8:34; Luke 9:23.

Again and again our Lord says, "Fear not, it is I."[170] If you always try to follow Him and administer His mercy, you need not be afraid; for He will always be there and always be saying, "Fear not, it is I."

God is terrible, and you must pray every day the prayer of sorrow. But He is also the Divine Compassion, and if you try to follow Him every day as best you can, and have the will to go on trying to follow Him so long as He may will you to remain, then you must have a humble confidence as well. "They shall obtain mercy."

The Gospel life of Peter begins with the summons to follow his Master; and it is with the same summons, "Follow me," that his life in the Gospel ends. The same is true of every Christian: he is summoned and empowered to follow through the grace of Baptism, anointed with oil for the journey at Confirmation, and given the daily bread of strength in the Eucharist, and at the end the summons will come again.

It is right that we should pray every day for the grace to be spared a sudden and unprovided death, but even this we must try to leave to His will. For the essential thing is to fear His justice, but to lift up our hands to His mercy; to sorrow and struggle but to trust. And so, at the end, if we have really tried to follow always and not to flag, He will tell us to follow Him once again, but to follow Him this time with joy to His eternal dwelling, to the glory and light and peace of the everlasting hills.

[170] Cf. Matt. 14:27; Mark 6:50.

Chapter Eight

Blessed are the clean of heart, for they shall see God.

Matt. 5:8

A. The Meaning of this Beatitude

Cleanness of heart

We have been thinking of the definition of happiness, first in terms of things you have (riches, comfort, and so on); then in terms of things that you do (the active life). There remains the question of the contemplative life, the life of vision. This, St. Thomas explains, is not to be found in the first half of any of the beatitudes since it is not the condition of acquiring happiness but is itself happiness. What you do find in these last two beatitudes is those effects of the life of action which immediately dispose a man to the life of vision: the quality whereby a man is made perfect in himself for the life of vision, and the quality whereby he is made perfect in his relations with his fellowmen. The first of the two is cleanness of heart.

Cleanness of heart involves temperateness

Let us think, to begin with, of what this means in the context of the moral life. We are concerned with the virtue of temperateness. The word has become attenuated and degraded in our modern speech, and the nature of the virtue has been seriously misunderstood. It is not synonymous with total abstention from alcohol, nor is it, in any case, restricted to a right use of food and drink. Most important, it is not simply a negative thing, a restraint, but a positive and creative quality, an essential quality of love.

Temperateness makes us reverent toward creatures

Temperateness has two aspects. First, it is what gives the qualities of humility and reverence to our attitude toward material things. It is what enables us to love things instead of grabbing, mauling, and battening on them; it is what enables us to contemplate and not to devour.

You can see an example of what this means (although the example itself is not necessarily an act of the virtue of temperateness) in the reverence with which a man who is alive to beauty will treat a glass of rare wine. The Christian virtue of temperateness differs from this because the motive is different — not the appreciation of beauty as an end in itself, but the curbing and training of the appetites for the love of God and His justice and therefore the restoring of the rule of spirit over flesh.

It remains true that Christian temperateness is essentially a humility of the flesh toward material things. As we saw in the first chapter, they are not just means to man's pleasure. They are of value in themselves as the handiwork of God, created to glorify Him, and so we have to learn to love them without greed and treat them without irreverence.

Moreover, in the Christian economy of life, things have an additional dignity: they are meant to receive a share of the blessing which flows from the redemptive power of Christ.

They are to be, in a sense, sanctified in themselves, and so to form a part of that process of total restoration whereby the world as a whole is led back to God. (So we say grace before meals; and so in the Church's ritual you find a form of blessing for all the material things which minister to the life of man.) You must treat them, then, with additional reverence, since there is this much holiness in them.

Then thirdly, there is the thought of the universal Providence of God. The least of these things which come into our lives and minister to us must be regarded not simply as ministering to a pleasure which implies no further purpose or responsibility, but, on the contrary, as the instrument, however small, of an eternal provision for an eternal destiny, and, in the end, as a part of God's eternal design for the world as a whole.

And fourthly, there is the glory of the omnipresence of God Himself in all His creatures, so your reverence for them must be a part of your reverence for Him who makes them His habitation.

And when you think not of material things in general, but of the bodies of men and women, then your reverence must be immeasurably intensified. For this is the flesh which in Christ was raised to the Godhead, and which thenceforward is in itself forever glorified. And it is the flesh in which the Godhead, the indwelling Trinity, resides in a special and intimate sense, so that those who have this presence within them are really one with the Godhead they adore. Therefore to treat them with irreverence is to be irreverent to God.

But you can only learn this Christian reverence for creatures by learning the second aspect of temperateness. The body needs to be chastised and beaten into subjection. To be temperate is to have learned, not to kill desires, but to control them. Here the virtue involves a constant daily discipline, a constant denial of the autonomous desires of the senses in order to affirm the rule of the spirit over a unified personality. Temperateness, and all the virtues which are part of it or connected with it (chastity, sobriety, gentleness, modesty, and the rest), train and subdue the passions of man so that instead of being masters enslaving the soul, they may become what they are intended by God to be: a part of the total unified drive which is man's journey to God.

Temperateness enlarges our very being

It is temperateness which makes us reverent, and thus it is not temperateness but its opposite which is negative and implies a lack of being. If you lack temperateness, you lack reverence, and therefore you cannot love. And you suffer this lack whenever you grab and domineer and do violence. You cannot love, but are restricted to a partial, because selfish and sensual, pleasure.

Love is a total enhancement of being, a glorifying of the whole body-spirit, because it is essentially a vital oneness with what is good and lovely. Temperateness, therefore, safeguards and perfects the life of the senses and therefore of the whole personality. The purpose of the life of the senses is to enable us to know, love, and become one with God's creatures — all of God's creatures, but human beings especially — and through them to be led to God, and so to have our own being immeasurably enlarged. Intemperateness is the denial of this enlargement of being, because the refusal of reverence means the refusal to regard things as objects of love (with the measure of equality and reciprocity which all love implies) and to substitute for this relationship of two-in-unity a purely one-sided utilization. Because it is purely one-sided, there is no enlargement of being: the self remains enclosed completely in its own narrow selfhood; and as long as it is intemperate, as long as it refuses to learn to be reverent, it can never break its bonds.

The intemperate man thus does a threefold violence: to himself, his own nature, since he is made to love and therefore to be made whole; to creatures as things in themselves, worthy of reverence, contemplation, and love; and to God, who gives this value to creatures, is present with them, and loves what He has made. To be intemperate is to be a destroyer.

But to be temperate is to fulfill: it is not to destroy passion or the delight of the senses in material things, but to fulfill them by fulfilling their nature. You do not love less, but more, when you treat them reverently as the wine lover treats his wine. You do not love less, but more, when your passion is ordered and controlled by reverence, for then it is glorified and intensified by being the vehicle of the life and power of the spirit. And you turn it into what, of its very nature, it is intended to be: an organic element in the total process of enlargement of the whole body-spirit, a means to forging the oneness of two beings, and a part of the shared life of love, worship, and service of God.

Temperateness gives our lives unity

Temperateness, then, is first of all the condition of the deep personal union of the self with other beings. But it is more than that. If the greatest reason for your reverence is your sense of God's presence in creatures, if you have learned thus to see things aright by seeing God within them, then you learn to make your whole life a unity — not an agglomerate of unconnected interests, but a single and all-inclusive fire. You learn to make all desires the different aspects and expressions of a single desire, the desire to serve God.

Then you will be clean of heart, and fit to see God, because you will have learned to love nothing apart from Him. By restoring its function to the life of the senses and making it a harmonious element in the total life of the body-spirit (not destroying the body to liberate the soul, but liberating the body from the separateness of lust and greed so that it may really be the partner of the soul), you will have achieved integrity and wholeness, and so restored something at least of the power of vision.

And you will be a little more worthy of the life of Heaven because you will incidentally have achieved beauty: that "shining forth of spirit through matter" which transforms and glorifies matter — the shining and transforming beauty which you find always in the faces of the saints.

Cleanness of heart includes purity of mind

You will have achieved, also, that purity of mind which is the second meaning of cleanness of heart. For the four cardinal virtues (prudence, temperateness, fortitude, and justice) are, in a sense, aspects of all virtuous action: there is a temperateness of the mind which corresponds to the temperateness of the flesh, a temperateness in regard to truth.

You are intemperate if you do violence to truth by trying to make it simply a means to your profit or pleasure; you are intemperate if you twist and pervert it. All forms of wishful thinking and self-deception, all of the ways in which you compromise and whittle away the truth, and every lack of candor — to yourself, to other men, to God — are forms of intemperateness of mind.

So are the ways in which we do violence in our thought to the nature of divinity: the anthropomorphisms, the projections of human emotions and limitations onto the Divine Nature, and the tendency to forget the justice of God and the need of awe in the face of the terrible, and to take refuge in a sentimental and humanitarian picture of His mercy.

Intemperate, too, are debased sentimental forms of piety and worship: the ways in which we turn worship into a sort of self-indulgence, pandering to emotions instead of lifting them up into a total act of worship of the whole body-spirit, which both expresses and strengthens the will, and fixes the gaze not on ourselves but on the reality of God. And you find in this self-indulgent parody of worship the same elements of irreverence, selfishness, and sensuality that you find in the intemperateness of the flesh. Instead of enhancement of the whole being, you have the isolated and therefore self-destructive indulgence of a part of the being; instead of a relationship of love, you have the isolation of the soul in its own selfhood, and the attempt to treat God as a utility; instead of the oneness with all creation which is in true worship, you have the ignoring of everything but the desires of the self.

This is not the way to cleanness of heart, but the way *from* it. It is the negation of vision, for you are not concerned to look at anything but to indulge yourself; you make the heart blind and opaque and gross because you make it turgid and muddy.

We can become clean of heart through the Liturgy

We can see the way to cleanness of heart if we look at the Church's Liturgy, for indeed if its first and supreme purpose is to give worship to God, it has the additional purpose of cleansing the mind and heart and the whole personality. Rather we should say that its purpose is to cleanse the personality so that then we may be able to offer God a more adequate sharing in the worship of Christ.

The Liturgy is art, but its essential material is man himself. The various arts of man, and all the creatures of the earth, and the sun and moon and stars, are brought into the act of worship; but it is first and foremost the total man (in Christ) who is self-offered, the total man who is expressed, and the total man who is cleansed.

For the Liturgy is both the revealing expression of the divine reality and man's response to it. And as the reality is expressed in sensible form and symbol, in rational statement, and in terms of the good which calls to the heart, so the response is the total response of senses, intuition, reason, and feeling (including both the emotions and the will). Song, gesture, and movement are the body's part in the total self-offering, and that offering includes the response of all the senses to the reality expressed. Life is given to this outward worship by the offering of mind and heart, raised to God in and through it, and again, that self-offering of spirit includes the response of reason to the rational formulas of faith, of intuition to their symbolic expression, and of emotion and will to those other aspects of the truth which we call the good and the beautiful.

In the offering and expression of the total man, the total man is also cleansed. The Liturgy is sacramental art: it effects what it signifies. This is, of course, true primarily of the sacraments themselves, but it is true in a broader sense of the whole of the Liturgy: the evoking of this response from the worshiper is itself a purification of the worshiper and a process whereby he is assimilated to the reality revealed.

Think of some very simple example: the lighted candle, for instance, which is part of so much of the Church's worship. There is food there for reason, for endless meditation: we know that the candle expresses worship, and the worship of love; it expresses the single-mindedness of the true Christian, whose whole life is to be an ascending flame of worship to God. We need not neglect the utilitarian aspect of the flame, for its purpose is to give light to other things, and so is ours (we remember that it was said of John the Baptist, "He was a burning and shining light"[171]). The candle is carried for the reading of the Gospel, which is the Light expressed in words, the words of the Word who is Light eternal; and our worship will be whole, and useful to the world, when it is wholly united with the self-offering of that same light which shines in the darkness.

With all this and much more we can fill the reasoning mind. And in so filling it we purify it, and we give direction to

[171] John 5:35.

all the other thoughts which follow when the moment of worship is over and, if we are faithful, we turn them also into worship.

But what reasoning can thus work out step by step, intuition can seize immediately, more dimly, perhaps, but more deeply: I am to be that candle; I am to be light and fire in Christ. And there follows the upward movement of will, desire, and feeling, for this Godward movement is, in fact, the fulfillment of the heart's perhaps unrecognized desire, and therefore is felt as good and desirable and to be achieved. So it is that the symbolism of the Liturgy can work in us even unconsciously, even if rationally we do not understand it: it can form the soul to its own pattern, until in the end, the pattern is expressed in the life of thought and action.

And finally the senses themselves are purified and perfected: you cannot live constantly with debased art without running the risk of being debased yourself, unless your awareness and your criticism ceaselessly react against it. Similarly you cannot live constantly with this God-revealing art without being turned gradually into worship. The burning light and the tall, white cylinder of wax, the purity of form and purpose, are a purgation for vision muddied by other appeals in which matter is isolated from spirit and degraded, and therefore turned to negation.

The Liturgy gives us integrity in three ways

The Liturgy is the worship of the total man; it is also and above all the worship of the *totus Christus*, "the total Christ," in whom the voice of all creation speaks. The Liturgy is cosmic art. The reality revealed is the answer to the age-old dreams of the universe, of that creation which is in travail even till now; and it is both a response and offering and a cleansing, for this returning of the universe to the Life is itself a renewal of life, a healing, a sanctifying, and a blessing.

So, if you learn through the Church's Liturgy to be clean of heart, you do three things: you achieve a personal integrity through a worship which is neither rational nor emotional but total, and therefore a total renewal of the self; you recover something of the integrity of the self in the cosmic family, and share in some degree in bringing back the cosmos to its Source; and you respond to that divine power which will give you the essential integrity without which nothing else is of importance: the integrity of the self in the infinity of God.

Cleanness of heart gives us greater spiritual vision

"They shall see God." We will turn later to the gift of the Spirit which, working not least through our reverent response to the Liturgy, gives us a far deeper penetration and clarity of mind. But let us here remember what will then be more emphatically verified: to be clean of heart is to be as a child, to have the clearness of eye of the child and the reverent docility toward reality that goes with it. Unless you are willing to accept reality as it is, and to reverence it for what it is, you cannot be clean of heart and mind.

We have, therefore, to pray for that docility; we have to pray that detachment, meekness, mourning, the hunger for God's justice, and the power of compassion may all together give us that temperateness toward things and toward truth which will recover for us our power of vision, and so make us fit for the Vision.

It is more to see God, says St. Thomas, than to sit at His table; "just as he is the greater man at court who not only dines but sees the king's countenance."[172] Self-centeredness and the lust which expresses it make us blind and take the life from us. If we want to be happy, we must learn to see God and His creatures as they are in themselves, and for their own sakes: we must pray all our lives the prayer of the man in the Gospel: "Lord, that I may see."

[172] *Summa Theologica*, I-II, Q. 69, art. 4.

B. The Gift of this Beatitude

The prayer of wonder and the gift of understanding

Now it came to pass, when He drew nigh to Jericho, that a certain blind man sat by the wayside begging. And he cried out, saying, "Jesus Son of David have mercy on me." And Jesus asked him, saying: "What wilt thou that I do to thee?" But he said: "Lord, that I may see." Jesus said to him: "Receive thy sight; thy faith hath made thee whole." And immediately he saw and followed Him, glorifying God.[173]

St. Paul, when he is writing to the Corinthians, makes a sharp distinction between the wisdom of this world and the wisdom of the Spirit. "It is written," he says, "*I will destroy the wisdom of the wise*. For the foolishness of God is wiser than men; and the weakness of God is stronger than men. The foolish things of the world hath God chosen that He may confound the wise: and the weak things of the world hath God chosen that He may confound the strong."[174] And again St. Paul says, "We speak the wisdom of God in a mystery, a wisdom which is hidden . . . which none of the princes of this world knew. For if they had known it, they would never have

[173] Luke 18:35, 38, 40-43.

[174] 1 Cor. 1:19, 25, 27.

crucified the Lord of glory."[175] And when he is speaking of the unknown things that God has prepared for those that love Him, he says, "But to us God hath revealed them, by His Spirit. For the Spirit searcheth all things, yea, the deep things of God."[176]

Divine wisdom and human wisdom are not incompatible

We are not to suppose that St. Paul is here setting the wisdom which is "from above"[177] in opposition to such wisdom as men can acquire by the right use of the mind, as though the two things were incompatible. It is not these two which are incompatible. In the great saints who were also great thinkers, you can distinguish four wisdoms: philosophy, theology, faith, and the wisdom which comes directly from the Spirit. They are distinct, they are different kinds of wisdom, but they do not clash.

St. Paul is speaking of those who are "wise according to the flesh,"[178] of the "princes of *this* world" (which, again, in the gospel sense is the world of darkness, of Satan, of mammon and pride), of the "sensual man."[179] In other words, we have here simply an application of that general contrast which we have been considering all along: the world unredeemed and

[175] 1 Cor. 2:7-8.
[176] 1 Cor. 2:10.
[177] James 3:15.
[178] 1 Cor. 1:26.
[179] Jude 1:19.

therefore still in the power of evil and darkness, the self which tries to be independent of God; and on the other hand, the world redeemed and therefore repentant and docile to the Spirit and receptive of the power of the Spirit, the self which has been reborn and has the Life within it, and can learn the truth from the Truth.

Philosophy, in this new life, does not lose its glory, but part of its glory is to recognize its limitations and admit that there are mysteries it can never fathom. Faith and theology can tell us immeasurably more, and the things they tell us are immeasurably more important. But even so, we see "as in a glass darkly,"[180] for the object of faith is in itself obscure: it is not yet the vision face to face to which it aspires.

The deeper wisdom is given to those who are docile enough to receive it. And the mind which can be quickened by the Spirit pierces — not by direct vision indeed but by a vital experience — even to the profundities of God, not only learning about the things of God but actually living them in the depths of the heart.

Understanding is knowledge of the heart

St. Thomas tells us that this understanding is an "intimate knowledge," for in two ways it differs from abstract rational knowledge: it pierces to the heart of things, and it is itself the heart's knowledge, the knowledge that is born of love.

How can love be said to know? Because when a thing is loved, it becomes in a special sense, as the old theologians

[180] 1 Cor. 13:12.

used to say, "connatural" to the lover: it is immediately *experienced.* You know a great deal *about* the thing you love, but if you put down on paper all that you know, you do not really touch on the essential, precisely because the essential is something that will not be put down in rational terms. Love is rightly said to know because the experience which is love becomes itself a part of the object, and so the mind knows the object precisely as loved and as experienced. You know the same thing, but you know it in a different way. You are beyond the realm of knowledge about things: you are in the realm of that *connaissance toute cordials*, that knowledge of the heart, which, because it is a direct experience, is a union not only of mind with its object but of the whole being with the thing loved.

When you apply this to the things of faith, its importance is obvious. We know as in a glass darkly; we know much about God through the mercy of His self-revelation, but this revelation is necessarily expressed for us in human terms, the terms of the creeds and doctrinal formularies. We are still obliged, therefore, to know the Creator through created things and created words. Because of this inadequacy, because of the immeasurable distance between this human expression of the reality and the reality itself, there arises first the danger of error and false interpretations; and secondly there is the inevitable dissatisfaction of the mind which always aspires to vision. "I sought Him whom my soul loveth: I sought Him, and I found Him not."[181] So the gifts of the Spirit are given, to overcome in some degree the obscurity of faith.

[181] Song of Sol. 3:1.

We are not yet concerned with the gift of wisdom, which takes the soul straight to the (still hidden) Godhead. The gift of knowledge enables us to judge — not by a process of reasoning but by a sort of inspired experience, so that a man *feels* rather than *judges* the truth of his conclusions — about what is and is not to be believed. Now we are concerned with understanding: that God-given experience which penetrates to the depths of the mysteries as revealed to us in human terms. And the first way in which this is achieved shows us the connection between this gift and the quality of cleanness of heart.

Sensory images can misrepresent God

The discipline of philosophy consists in training the mind to see and investigate immaterial reality without being misled by sensory images. In the same way the drawing near of the mind to God demands an emancipation from the sensory images, the anthropomorphisms, which must otherwise lead it astray. "We shall know God the more perfectly in this life," says St. Thomas, "insofar as we understand more and more how He surpasses everything the intellect can comprehend."

It is, of course, essential to distinguish this *via negativa* of the men of prayer — the setting aside, when searching for God in prayer, of all distraction from sensory images, from created reality, in order to arrive at the cloud of unknowing in which the Godhead itself is sensed — from the way of rejection as a total attitude toward life. As a Christian, as we have seen, you are inevitably concerned with created things: you are part of the world that God has made, and you have a duty toward it; you cannot love God if you refuse to love your neighbor. But here we are concerned, not with our attitude toward the world, but with the question of how to pray, and it is clear that if we are to set our minds to search for God, we must first try to free them (during prayer) from all things which would impede them in their quest: the cares, anxieties, preoccupations of our daily life in general, and in particular the sensory images which misrepresent the Godhead.

"When thou shalt pray," our Lord tells us, "enter into thy chamber and, having shut the door, pray to thy Father in secret."[182] He is speaking primarily against ostentation; but His words are also the perfect symbol of this ascent of the soul to God. "We must remember," says St. John of the Cross, "that the Word, the Son of God, together with the Father and the Holy Spirit, is hidden in essence and presence in the inmost being of the soul. The soul, therefore, that will find Him must go out from all things in will and affection and enter into the profoundest self-recollection, and all things must be to it as if they existed not.

"Hence St. Augustine saith: 'I found Thee not without, O Lord; I sought Thee without in vain, for Thou art within.' . . . Seeing, then, that the Bridegroom whom thou lovest is the treasure hidden in the field of thy soul, for which the wise merchant gave all that he had, so thou, if thou wilt find Him, must forget all that is thine, withdraw from all created things, and hide thyself in the secret retreat of the spirit, shutting the door upon thyself — that is, denying thy will in all things — and praying to thy Father in secret. Then thou, being hidden

[182] Matt. 6:6.

within Him, wilt be conscious of His presence in secret, and wilt love Him, possess Him in secret, and delight in Him in secret, in a way that no tongue or language can express."

Happy, then, are the clean of heart because, in the first place, they have learned to reverence all things in and for God, so that their minds and hearts are not always being led away from Him, but, on the contrary, are always being drawn to Him. Happy, in the second place, because they can be led by the Spirit into this secret place apart and be undistracted by senses and imaginings, and so can learn to search even the profundities of God.

In moments of quiet, we discover God's presence

To be undistracted, unperturbed: you find in theologians and mystics alike a constant emphasis on the idea of *quiet*. The gift of understanding, the theologians tell us, gives the soul a sense of the certitude of the things of faith; of the inner meaning of the scriptural account of the divine mysteries; and of the infinite perfection of God and the nothingness of man, which bring it *quiet*. And the mystics describe the effects of this gift precisely in terms of the "prayer of quiet."

"There came to me in this *quiet*," says St. Teresa, "the delightful discovery of the hidden sense in the Psalms and the Scriptures." And again: "The soul then receives communication concerning the great truths. . . . Without seeing the Master so full of kindness who teaches her, she *knows that He is near her*."

It is that quiet sense of the near presence of Him in whom are all things, and the quiet sense of certitude which the presence brings, that this gift establishes in the prayerful soul. That is why it is so immensely important that we should set aside some time every day — half an hour if we can possibly manage it; a quarter of an hour at the very least — for the purpose of learning to pray thus in secret, learning to be quiet in the presence, and so to acquire all through the day a "sense of our last end."

In the prayer of wonder, we adore God

We have been thinking, previously, of the prayer of awe, the prayer of filial reverence, the prayer of petition, and the prayer of sorrow. Here we come to the lovely prayer of wonder: the still, wordless gaze of adoration which is proper to the lover. You are not talking, not busy, not worried or agitated; you are not asking anything: you are *quiet*, you are just *being with*, and there is love and wonder in your heart. So this prayer is indeed a beginning of beatitude; for the heart is filled and is content simply to be — and its being is all adoration.

You find some hint of this utterly serene but utterly humble sense of infinity in some of the greatest music: in some of Bach or of César Franck,[183] for example, or of the Beethoven of the last quartets, or again in Wolf's *Ganymed*. You find it in the music of the Mass, when the *Alleluia* traces its pattern of sound on the last vowel, saying nothing, yet saying everything. You find it expressed in the words of the Apostle Thomas, abashed at his unbelief: "My Lord and my God!"[184]

[183] French composer (1822-1890).
[184] John 20:28.

But let us note three points of great importance. First, this is a prayer to which we must aspire; but the way of prayer is long and hard, and we have to begin at the beginning. Nor should we suppose that only this prayer of quiet can give us a constant sense of God's presence, and of our last end: any sincere prayer will gradually do that, although the prayer of quiet will do it more forcibly and more fully.

Secondly, the prayer of quiet will never supersede the simplicities of the Our Father: we never get beyond the need of awe, fear, sorrow, and petition. This prayer may be given to us at moments, and if we grow in wisdom, the moments will be longer and more frequent; that is all.

And thirdly, it is true that in the prayer of quiet you ask nothing; you simply adore. But this adoration is never an indifference to the fate of the world, of your brethren: you shut the door and pray in secret; you "forget all that is yours and withdraw from all created things" so that your mind and heart may leap up to God; but because you have charity in you, the needs and sorrows of these created things go silently with you, they are part of you, and the blessing with which you return is a blessing in which they must necessarily share. Your love of God still includes your love of your family.

Understanding lets us see God's beauty in creatures

And as we saw in the last section, it is precisely this same sort of attitude which the virtue of temperateness teaches us to adopt toward all created things, as part of our reverence for God. For them, too, you must learn to feel wonder, provided always that you guard yourself against isolating their beauty from its Maker. And here, too, perhaps the gift of understanding has its purpose: since it can teach us to go to the heart of things and to learn the heart's knowledge even where no beauty is apparent, even where there is stupidity and sin. It can teach us to go beyond a perhaps unattractive, perhaps repulsive exterior, to the presence of God within. It can teach us to reverence the pain and the ugliness of the world, for in these, too, the love-mercy of God is implicit.

It can, therefore, lead us to the prayer of gratitude. There are problems which only the heart's knowledge, piercing to the heart of things where God's compassion abides, can solve; and to solve them is to be grateful to God, for the solution is the compassion. This prayer, too, at its highest and best, is part of the wordless prayer of wonder and adoration, for the deepest wonder is aroused not simply by Beauty in itself, but by Beauty stooping to comfort ugliness because of the compassion which is love.

The prayer of wonder is not, like the prayer of petition, primarily a means to something: it is an end in itself, it is life, and the beginning of beatific life. But you cannot pray this prayer without its overflowing into action, the sort of action that saves, heals, and consoles. And because of the twofold meaning of cleanness of heart, the converse is also true: the more your service of the world grows in reverence and love, and the more the virtue of temperateness draws your love of all things into the unity of your love of God, so also the more you will grow in cleanness of heart's knowledge and therefore in wonder, and the more you will be made worthy to see and praise God in the final fulfillment of vision of the heavenly home.

C. The Sacrament of this Beatitude

Marriage

And the wine failing, the mother of Jesus saith to Him: "They have no wine." . . . Jesus saith to them: "Fill the waterpots with water." And they filled them up to the brim.[185]

Christianity is the creed of acceptance. You must not dally with Manicheism, the worst of heresies: you must never think that some of the things that God has made are good and to be accepted, while others are evil in themselves. The gracious miracle at Cana is our Lord's affirmation of the goodness of material things — His approval of wine, gaiety, and good-fellowship, and of the vocation of marriage.

They filled them up to the brim: the first thing is to accept the gift of life with both hands from God; and that includes the full acceptance of human nature, of the unity of the body-spirit.

But there is also the other side. To be a full acceptance of life, it must be an acceptance, also, of the fact of sin. You accept the wholeness of human nature and its essential goodness, but you realize that sin has twisted it and turned it to evil.

[185] John 2:3, 7.

And so you have to safeguard your affirmation from becoming an idolatry; and you have, in particular, to safeguard your joy in material things from becoming isolated from the governance of the spirit. Material things are to be reverenced for what they are. They are not just utilities. On the other hand, it is part of their nature to fulfill a function, and it is part of the reverence we owe them to remember that function.

In marriage, man and woman are fulfilled

Sex in man is essentially different from sex in animals, because its function is different. It is not a purely biological thing: it is much greater than that. Of its nature it is also part of that process whereby the oneness of two human beings is achieved; and that oneness itself is meant to be a means whereby the two human beings together become one with God. Human marriage is the most complete fulfillment of the part the body may play in the union of spirit with spirit, and may thus become, too, the ground of the union of this two-in-unity with infinite Spirit.

They filled them up to the brim. There is nothing niggardly or half-hearted about this Christian acceptance of the flesh; and the acceptance of the body's function is the acceptance of the fullness of human love. But as we have seen, you need the virtue of temperateness, not to deny or to destroy, but, on the contrary, to fulfill: and you fulfill precisely insofar as you avoid both idolatry and sensuality by making sex part of the totality of love, and love part of the totality of worship.

Man is essentially a creator. Married love is normally the primary fulfillment of men and women because normally it is the primary form of creation. "And the Lord God said: It is not good for man to be alone."[186] The individual is incomplete: in body, mind, heart, and will; and in the normal way of things, it is through the love of men and women for each other that this manifold completeness comes. And the creation of new life is both the expression of that completeness (for now it is the new thing, the new unity, which is creative and outward-turning) and also the means whereby the completeness is achieved (for the unity not only of the flesh but of mind and heart as well is made through this making). Similarly with the worship of God: it is the two who are now one who express and glorify their oneness in worship, but worship is also the highest means whereby their oneness is established and made eternally secure.

Christianity raises marriage to a greater dignity

Christianity, then, so far from condemning sex or regarding it as something shameful or something to be apologized for, raises it, together with the whole man of whom it is a function, to a new dignity: first, inasmuch as it is an element in the normal means whereby men and women are to worship God in fullness of life; secondly, because it is part of that vocation of marriage which our Lord has raised to the dignity of a sacrament, with all that implies of supernatural greatness.

To that greatness we shall return in a moment. Let us first of all think of the sacrament in terms of the special needs it is destined to meet.

[186] Gen. 2:18.

Marriage is a lifework

Marriage is a great vocation, is indeed the normal human vocation; but a vocation is a lifework, and to think of it in these terms is, therefore, to be on our guard against romanticizing it and forgetting its true nature. It is a lifework because it is something that takes a lifetime to achieve. You have first of all the making of the unity of man and woman; and this is itself an endless process. On the physical level there is need of gentle adjustment of the two wills so that there may be real peace and fulfillment. In the sphere of mind there is the long and laborious process, not indeed of coming to agree on every conceivable issue, but of reaching a real and stable sympathy of mind, a real unity on great issues, and a real mutual complementing of the two different ways of thought. Finally there has to be the unity of the deep personal will (not that there can ever be a complete agreement of desire in every superficial and transient issue), so that beneath the surface differences, there may be a solid core of unity which nothing can shake. All this is not achieved in a day or a year.

Nor is the making of the family, and of the life of the family, which is both the purpose of the unity of man and woman and the means to it. And here, especially, we have to be careful not to romanticize: the stuff of married life is the daily work, the daily drudgery; all the burdens which the care of children involves; the economic anxieties; the responsibilities; and finally the selflessness which knows and accepts the time when the unity of the family has to be split up, and the new generation must go forth and make its own life and its own families.

Unless all this can be recognized as the essence of marriage, there is bound to be disaster. There is the deep, underlying joy, the long happiness of comradeship, and the moments of glory: these, too, are essential, for they are love, and it is love which turns drudgery into joy. But if you try to isolate the glamour and forget the labor, if you think of marriage as an endless, carefree honeymoon, then you are distorting its nature, and you will be very unhappy.

That is the first reason why we are given this sacrament: to help us to make marriage a *life*, a life in which the hard work is never eluded but fully accepted and turned by the power of love into something creative — the creation of goodness and happiness, the creation of worship.

They filled them up to the brim. When you accept the reality of marriage thus with both hands and in its wholeness, and refuse to deceive yourself into thinking that glamour is all, then the power of the sacrament will make your love strong and lasting and the means of a closer and closer union with God. It will do more than that. The family is meant to be creative of more than itself.

Marriage helps to create the life of the Church and of the world

The first glory of parenthood is that man and woman become, in the words of a pope, the "ministers of God's omnipotence," sharing with Him in the tremendous work of making immortal human beings. But they are also the symbol of the union of Christ and His Church; and that union, too, is a creative thing, from which the power and victory of good in the world proceed. To love together is to create worship; to worship together is to create love; but to love and worship as one is to help in the creating of the life of the Church. The new unity looks beyond itself to the life of the family, the home; but the home, in its turn, must look beyond itself to the world without.

Apply here what we have been thinking of in earlier chapters: the spirit of poverty, meekness, mourning, and the rest, the spirit of loving and creative sacrifice: you have in the love which can give itself to and for the child a symbol of — and more than that, an introduction to — the sacrificial life of love of the Christian in the world. The family, in its turn, must give itself to and for the world. It must be for the world a visible demonstration of the religion of love; and that it will be, first by its own unity and peace; but the unity and peace must turn outward, must radiate love and light and the homage of service, so that the home may be not only something that others can admire, but a hearth to which they can always come and be welcome, and sit and be warm.

Unmarried persons are also called to family service

Marriage is thus the normal way, not only in which men and women become whole in themselves, not only in which they love and worship God, but also in which they serve the Church and the world.

And those whose vocation is not to married life? They can be in a yet higher state, if they choose the life of virginity for the love of God, if they forgo the good things of family life in order to know, love, serve God more fully and more intensely.

And the relevant point here is that the Church exalts this state of virginity not (as is too commonly supposed) because She disapproves of sex or human love or the family (the Church is indeed in these days almost the only surviving defender of family life), but precisely because She knows that this state of life is not a destruction of love, even of love of persons, but, on the contrary, is an immense enlargement and enrichment of it, a dedication to it.

Those in this state of life have their family, but it is a larger family, and one which is harder to serve. Some are called to the family life of the cloister: they have the same need to love and to be made whole by their love; the same need to see the building up of the life of their family as their primary lifework; the same need, therefore, to make the good of the family the criterion of what they do; the same need to go beyond justice, and see that the family life is built not on the bare minimum of justice but on the maximum of love. They lack the help of the physical love which can be so vast a driving force for making the unity of spirit; they lack the blood ties which can do so much to make the home a unity; they have special dangers: of order turning into starchy formalism, of authority being degraded into external regimentation and routine, and of love being destroyed by divisions, incompatibilities, and prejudices.

But they have, too, their special graces, and in addition, they escape some of the dangers of the smaller world of married life. They need not find their celibacy a subtraction of life, a disability to mind or body, if their energies are turned to the wider opportunities of their family life — all the creative work of the cloister itself, but also the creation of a wider and wider circle of love, compassion, and strengthening influence in the world about them. And as with the ordinary human home, so with the religious house: it is as a family, as a unity of love and worship, that it best can help in building the world outside. The individual can do much to draw men to Christ, but when you have a whole community which is a visible demonstration of the life of love in Christ, and of the loving invitation of Christ, then indeed you have a power in the land.

And still there are others whose vocation it is to live neither a married nor a community life: they, too, have their family, and it is immediately the world. Theirs can be the hardest vocation of all; for they must be all things to all men without the strength and solace of a smaller unity to complete them and make them happy. Such, for example, are the priests who do not live in community, although clearly they, too, in a sense, have their smaller family, the community immediately about them in their parish, which they have to labor to build into a unity of love and worship so that it, in its turn, may fulfill its family vocation in the greater world. And in the power of the priesthood, all the labor and drudgery of making and serving that family is turned to glory.

Such also are all those who give themselves in charity to a life of service of mankind — in nursing, art, and scientific research — and in order to do so the more fully, they deny themselves the comfort of a family life of their own.

We must accept all that our vocation involves

Whether, then, you think of married life, or of these other ways in which you have always to make and serve the life of a family, the same essential truth holds: you worship God by and in your making, and in your making, you yourself become whole; and each of the three things is the cause of the others: you make well if your making is worship; you worship well if you worship as a maker; and your making and your worship are what make you whole.

But the condition, too, is always the same. They filled them up to the brim: you accept your vocation in its fullness, the fullness of marriage and family life; of the shared life of any community; or of a life of sacrifice to humanity as a whole — not as an abstract but as the total family of individual men and women. Then, if your acceptance is the acceptance of love; if the drudgery is turned into an endless expression of love; if the family life you have fashioned turns outward to the larger world with all the power of love, and of love-in-unity, so that the circle of its healing influence grows wider and wider as the years go by, and the intensity of its love burns deeper and deeper, until you have conquered prejudices and limitations, and your house and your heart are always full — then, indeed, you will have filled your life to the brim in love and gratitude and service to Him who is Life to every man that cometh into the world. And in the power of His universal love and universal compassion, He will bless you, and the water will be turned into wine.[187]

[187] John 2:9.

Chapter Nine

Blessed are the peacemakers, for they shall be called the children of God.

Matt. 5:9

Love of peace

The quality in our relations with our fellowmen which immediately disposes us to the life of vision, says St. Thomas, is the love of peace. Why? Because the life of vision — the life of the quiet prayer of wonder and the greater prayer of union — is incompatible with agitation. You cannot adore the other in self-oblivion, you cannot "cast all your cares away," if you are tossed about on a sea of worries and solicitudes about external things, or if you are not yet at peace within the mind itself because of a lack of complete identity of will with the infinite Will. "Wisdom," says St. Augustine, "is to the peace-lovers, in whom there is no movement of rebellion, but obedience to Reason." But wisdom is the end.

Wisdom judges things in light of their ultimate cause

It is useful for man to have much information about matters of fact, but that is not wisdom. It is useful to have scientific knowledge, to know the immediate what and why of things, but that is not wisdom either. It is better to have philosophy, which is the knowledge of things not in their immediate but in their ultimate causes: that is wisdom, although it is not the highest form of wisdom. It is wisdom because it reduces the manifold of life to the one, and therefore makes things intelligible as a unity.

But to make the dry bones live,[188] you need the vision, the intuition or awareness, of things in all their concreteness, their goodness and beauty as well as their truth. Above all, you need some degree, at least, of direct knowledge of the nature of the one; and when you have *that* vision in its plenitude — the plenitude which, knowing something of God in Himself, sees all things in Him and Him in all things — and at the same time the wisdom which judges all things in the light of the highest of all causes, the Cause of all being Itself, then you have wisdom in the fullest and deepest sense. And seeing things, as it were, with the eyes of God, you share something of the peace of God.

Wisdom from above brings peace

That supreme wisdom, as we have seen, is "from above"; it is given to those who have the humility and the docility to receive it, to those who have learned to be as little children. Wisdom is given to those who are obedient to Reason.

That conformity is not a negation of freedom, a yoke upon the mind, but the liberation of the spirit from darkness into light; it is the joy, peace, and exhilaration of learning from Love. It is peace, in particular, because it brings with it a security — of the will as well as of the mind — which no

[188] Cf. Ezek. 37:1-10.

acquired wisdom can have. "And when they shall bring you into the synagogues and to magistrates and powers, be not solicitous how or what you shall answer, or what you shall say: for the Holy Spirit shall teach you in the same hour what you must say."[189] You are carefree, you cannot be racked with worry, your mind is at rest, because you have the untroubled vision and the docility of the child.

Wisdom shows us how to be peacemakers

Happy are the peacemakers. You cannot be a peacemaker among your brethren unless you are also acquiring some measure of peace in your own heart. You must be trying to live in what Augustine calls the *tranquillitas ordinis*: the tranquillity which comes of ordered desire — and desires are ordered when they are unified, when all desires are aspects of one single desire, and all loves are included in one universal love. You have the tranquillity of order, in other words, when you have within you the reintegration of God's order, when you are reborn in the Spirit and so made whole because you are restored to the status of a son of God. That is why the peace-lovers are happy: they shall be called the children of God.

The two things, wisdom and sonship, are related. Why? Because, says St. Thomas, it is wisdom which makes us like to Christ, who is the Wisdom begotten of the Father. All that mediatorship in Christ which we have been thinking of as the function of the Christian in the world, all the work the Christian must do to heal, comfort, strengthen, and restore

[189] Luke 12:11-12.

depends on wisdom. Goodwill is not enough. There must be the hunger and thirst to do; but there must be the wisdom which instructs us in what to do.

So you come back again to the child, whose vision is not clouded by prejudice, nor his judgment twisted by the pragmatisms of selfish profit or pleasure. It is a tragedy that our art, in its representations of the Wisdom begotten of the Father, has lost the tradition of the *Puer Aeternus*, the Eternal Boy, that Christian fulfillment of the conception of the youthful Apollo in his slender grace and supple strength of body, his clear and serene intellectuality, with the addition of the divine gentleness of the Shepherd. For this is the beauty that is ever old and ever new: ever old because there is in it the compassionate wisdom of all the ages of the world; ever new because there is in it the gracious receptivity of youth. Christ is the eternal Wisdom, but the eternal Wisdom begotten: we become like to Him, and therefore filled with His peace, when we learn from Him the age-old wisdom by learning to be as a child.

If we are thus, if through docility we are learning little by little to make all desires one desire, then we are beginning to be lovers and makers of peace in the world: we shall beget peace in the hearts of others not only by what we do and say, but by what we are. This beatitude is indeed the fruit of the preceding ones: for you will give to others if you are poor in spirit and not grasping; you will be humble and quiet if you are meek and you reverence creatures; you will be ready to bear others' burdens if you are of those who mourn because of their love and sympathy; you will remove strife if you hunger and thirst for God's justice, and still more if you are filled with divine mercy and compassion; and you will have power over others if you are clean of heart and mind. And then, finally, wisdom will tell you "how or what you shall answer and what you shall say"; wisdom will tell you — now eager to love, help, and serve — how to do it.

Wisdom and docility foster peace in the family

Let us think a little of what it means to be a peacemaker in the life of the family. It is wisdom that most fully and perfectly makes peace there, because wisdom removes the ultimate ground and occasion of those clashes of mind and will that arise too often from an inability to see the manifold in terms of the one, to see all secondary issues in terms of the final purpose of the home, which is the love and the glory of God.

But again, it is the quality of the child-life that makes peace in the home. Discord comes of stubborn self-assertion, and although you can say that this self-assertion is the defect of a quality (for you help to create the life of the family best if you can contribute something of your own, if you have initiative and a mind of your own), still it must remain a defect unless there goes with this power to create, the sense of the unity of the family and of the final purpose of the family — only, that is, if initiative is combined with docility to the laws which govern initiative.

You create peace in the home by being yourself at peace, although, of course, it is equally true that you learn to be at peace yourself by striving to bring peace to the home. You create joy by being yourself filled with joy. Again and again, we come back to the same principle: it is what you *are* that matters most.

The vocation of every Christian as such is to bring joy into the lives of those with whom he comes in contact, and, above all, into the life of his own home. But you cannot do this self-consciously; there is nothing more depressing than the empty, self-conscious bonhomie which is paraded as a studied program, and in no way reflects the state of mind and heart behind it. But even where there is real affection, goodwill is not enough: you need wisdom. There is such a thing as misplaced jocularity; there are times when it can be a social crime to be bonhomous at the breakfast table. You need understanding, you need a sense of what is right at a given moment, or your goodwill may lead to disaster. Some people have this social sense, and know by instinct what to do; others are less favored and must labor to acquire it; but all need the gift of wisdom, in any case, to unify their social life, to make all that they do a means not only to the immediate peace and well-being of the family, but to its final happiness in Heaven.

Peace is not found in mere agreeability or compromise

It is possible to confuse the establishment of real peace with a cowardly avoidance of all issues, just as it is possible to confuse love with unprincipled agreeability. You must labor and pray for that peace which the world cannot give, and you will find it, not in compromise, not in always giving way to the immediate desires of the moment for the sake of a quiet life, but only by establishing the condition of peace, which is charity.

And *charity* is not a vague term; it does not mean an easygoing amiability. On the contrary, it is a question of the will. Thou shalt love the Lord thy God; thou shalt love thy neighbor: in each case, to love is to will the good of the other. That is why love is sometimes superficially and apparently hard: you want the good of the other so much that you are prepared to see him suffer if necessary, however much it hurts him, and you.

Unity of desire brings peace

And so it is with peace. St. Thomas is quite clear: if you want peace within yourself, you must unify all desires, which means that you must make all desires the aspects of one single desire. This means, in its turn, that you must love — you must will to obey — God, above all things.

And if you want peace with and in your family, it is the same thing: you must want their good as much as you want your own; you must drive out selfishness, envy, jealousy, and spite, and learn the meaning of the love that serves. You will do this if you have the first kind of peace, because then you will see the good of the family as part of that will of God which it is your supreme desire to fulfill.

But to do that is to live in the present: you know and recognize the presence of God in the midst of your family, and His continuous Providence for it; you are at peace within yourself in the fullest sense because you are content to do the work of the present moment and let God provide for the future. "Be not solicitous":[190] it does not mean, of course, that you must take no thought at all for tomorrow; that is part of

[190] Matt. 6:25; Luke 12:11.

the vocation of family life. But it does mean that when you have taken all prudent measures and have done what you can with the means God has given you, then you refuse to worry, to be agitated, and to make yourself miserable with imagined future woes or present difficulties.

God has care of us: that is the visible demonstration of charity that you find in those Christian homes where the lovers and makers of peace abide, the people in whom the gifts of the Spirit shine in splendor. God has care of us: and therefore even though times are incredibly hard, and these people have to work all day and most of the night to make ends meet, and there seems never any security for the future, still they are filled with joy,[191] and with that peace the world cannot give.

Wisdom means the ability to take the long view about everything, and that is, again, why wisdom and peace go together. If you are hopelessly upset by every transient ill fortune; if you are thrown off your balance by every threat of trouble in the future, however remote; if you are endlessly worried about the state of your own soul and the perils which may beset it, instead of trying to love God and living in the trust which is begotten of love; then of course you are not at peace. But wisdom teaches you to look beyond these fears and

[191] Most of us, it is true, find that, not only great sorrow, but also ill health, drudgery, and fatigue can make any feeling of joy impossible for us. Yet even we can discover the difference between the blank despair which these things are capable of bringing upon us and the peace with which a sense of God's presence can alleviate them. And if we knew this presence as vividly as the saints do, we should know their unquenchable joy as well. "He who can bear suffering well," says Blessed Henry Suso, "receives in this world a portion of the reward of his sufferings, for he finds peace and joy in all things."

timidities to the great lines of the eternal design, and the great power, love, and protection of the everlasting arms. And then you have within you a peace which nothing can dismay, because you know that nothing can separate you from the charity of God which is in Christ Jesus our Lord.[192]

So it will be given you in that hour what you shall say — and not only in the times of crisis, when you are faced with some equivalent of synagogues and magistrates. It will be given you, if you have ears to hear, what you shall say and what you shall do always, at every hour and in all circumstances. You will have a social sense greater than that which some have by nature and others by hard-won experience; you will have a *divine* sense of what love demands, and you will bring joy into the lives of your brethren because you will be filled with the glowing light of the Godhead.

Wisdom enables us to live in God's eternal present

The gift of wisdom, then, enables us to act not only in the power but in the wisdom of Christ. It is this wisdom, this sense of the nearness of the guiding hand of God, which explains the much misunderstood doctrine of "indifference" and "abandonment to the will of God." If you take these without the burning love and divine wisdom that make them positive and creative things, you distort and indeed destroy them.

"Teach us to care and not to care." First you must have the love which embraces all things, but which sees things aright, in God: you must live, and love, in the present. We live in the

[192] Rom. 8:39.

world of time, in which things are ceaselessly fading and passing away, and the insecurity of the presence of what we love lies heavy upon us.

But that is only one side of the picture. Things which in themselves are fleeting exist also in the mind of God, and in the mind of God they eternally abide. For the life of God is the eternal "now": the single infinite moment in which there is neither past nor future, but all things are equally and forever present. We, for our part, must see the tapestry of time piece-meal, as though we walked along beside it and could see only the part immediately before our eyes; but the eyes of God see the thing simultaneously in its wholeness, so that events which to us are remote in the past or unpredictable in the future are to Him no more remote or unreal than the actual moment of our temporal present. In the mind of God, then, we must not suppose that things come to be or pass away; we must not suppose that there the flower fades and ceases to exist or that the dead animal is as lost as it is to the world of time.

For us there is inescapably the torment of the finite mind; but we are given this gift of wisdom to help us to see *quasi oculo Dei*, as if with the eyes of God — that is, to have, in our own finite way, a dim perception of the way of the mind and the heart of God. And when we apply this to the world about us, it can give us courage and comfort for the tyranny of time. We cannot have God's vision of things, but we can know about it and realize that it means that there is a sense in which, when the flower fades and dies, it nonetheless has not wholly sunk into nothingness.

And so, when the things you love are taken from you, you need not be sunk in utter misery and despair, because in spite of your sorrow you know that they are not wholly lost; you know that in eternity nothing is lost; you know that if you could share the life of the eternal present, you would find them there in the infinite reality of the heart of God. And insofar as you learn to listen to, and to live by, the wisdom of the Spirit, you learn to think thus of things, precisely because you learn to see them and love them not apart from God but in God and for God. You learn to leave them to God, and to leave your love of them to God. It is all in His hands, they are in His hands, and you yourself are in His hands.

And so the transitoriness of earthly life begins to be, in a sense, a matter of indifference to you. This is not because you come to the soured conclusion that since nothing can last, nothing can matter. On the contrary, it is because you realize that things have all the importance of the eternal present, and that this importance confers on them a kind of abidingness which heals and consoles your spirit, and you have with your sorrow a peace and a joy which cannot be taken from you, where otherwise, perhaps, you would have only despair.

Abandonment to Providence is a positive act of will

It is the same with what is called (rather unfortunately in English) "abandonment to divine Providence." It is an unfortunate expression, because it suggests to us a purely negative and somber state of affairs. It means exactly the opposite.

It includes, first of all, the idea of a total loving acceptance of the will of God. We thought of this at the beginning of the book: the total destruction of self-will, the stripping of the self of all its independence and pride, and, on the other hand, the wholehearted acceptance of all that God wills for us because it *is* His will. This acceptance is not just a passive resignation in the ordinary colloquial sense of the word, but rather an active holding out of one's hands to God's will, a positive *willing*, and therefore an attitude of loving gratitude to God for all that He sends, whether it be joy or pain.

Therefore, for that very reason, this abandonment includes the idea that is implied in the word *abandon:* something entirely carefree, spontaneous, and without reserve in the sense, let us say, in which conventional reserve can shackle inspiration or gaiety. When you have the sense of God's Providence guiding every event, however insignificant, the conviction (begotten of wisdom) that all things work together unto good, and the humble childlike trust that if you love as much as you can and do the best you can, God will guide you in all your words and works, then of course you are abandoned to His will in the sense that you become free of fret or worry, you cast your care on God, and you do not scheme to circumvent His designs. On the contrary, you love and welcome all that He gives you precisely as His gift, whether pleasant or painful. You are poor and meek, you hunger for justice and are clean of heart, and your will is to do God's will because, through your love, you see God in all things and events. And therefore you have this element of "abandon" in the other sense: you are filled with joy and happiness because you are entirely carefree.

Peace and wisdom enable us to serve the whole world

To have this fullness of peace and wisdom is, of course, to serve more than the immediate family. By being thus, you will act always, because of what you are, in the wisdom and the power of Christ: you will act for the *totus Christus*, and for the whole family of mankind.

All that we were thinking before of mercy and compassion finds its fruition here: "To make peace, either in oneself or among others," says St. Thomas, "shows one to be a follower of God, who is the God of unity and peace."[193] You comfort — you console and strengthen — by making the world about you a world of peace. And this you can only do by learning gradually and with ceaseless travail to live wholly for God and in His love, so as, in the end, to let God shine forth from you, showing forth in yourself the peace of God, and thus bringing your brethren, perhaps in great multitudes down the ages, to the feet of Christ. But you can do this only by being a man of peace, and the way to that is prayer and humility, vision and love.

Love of peace is a fruit of compassion

It is a lovely epitaph to be called a peacemaker. Other greatness can win the honor of men; this greatness wins their love. And why? Perhaps it is because this greatness is essentially the fruit of compassion — for it is when you are very wise and humble that you can be compassionate, not before — and the divine compassion is what compels love. To be a lover and maker of peace is the vocation of every Christian as such.

But each beatitude depends on those which have gone before: you must be poor, meek, clean of heart, and merciful,

[193] *Summa Theologica*, I-II, Q. 69, art. 4.

and then you will have within you the will which is our peace. "The highest place in the royal palace," says St. Thomas, referring to the second half of this beatitude, "belongs to the king's son":[194] but let us remember that it was when he had thrown away everything and had wed the lady Poverty and fallen in love with all humanity and all reality in the immensity of God, and gone forth naked — abandoned, carefree — to serve them, that St. Francis sang his song of pride and joy and glory: I am a king's son.

[194] Ibid.

B. The Gift of this Beatitude

The prayer of union and the gift of wisdom

For wisdom is more active than all active things: and reacheth everywhere by reason of her purity. For she is a vapor of the power of God and a certain pure emanation of the glory of the almighty God. . . . And being but one she can do all things: and remaining in herself the same she reneweth all things. . . . She is more beautiful than the sun, and above all the order of the stars: being compared with light, she is found before it. For after this cometh night, but no evil can overcome wisdom.[195]

Wisdom is the deepest and the loveliest of the gifts. It marks, in a sense, the end of that process that we have been considering, the process which begins with the new birth in Baptism: the death of the false self, and the coming to be of the new self *in* God.

It marks, therefore, the summit of both the child-life and of the life of maturity: the child-life, because there is the complete fulfillment of this gift when the soul is completely rapt in God, completely restored to oneness; the mature life, because this is the gift which enables us to judge all things by their "highest causes" — it is the gift which, when it is completely active in a man, makes him a *sage*.

[195] Wisd. 7:24-25, 27, 29-30.

Sapientis est ordinate: it belongs to the wise man to put things in order. It belongs to the man who is wise with the wisdom of the Holy Spirit, the wisdom "from above," to put things in their divine order, bringing the entire manifold of creation into unity so that "all things work together for good," but doing so not with the violence of regimentation, but with divine reverence and compassion for the least of created things. For we are told of divine wisdom that she "reacheth from end to end mightily," but also that "she ordereth all things sweetly."[196]

Wisdom includes all of the Beatitudes

Wisdom is the end of the process because in wisdom all of the Beatitudes are included, and all those good things are present which, without wisdom, are misinterpreted so that men follow after strange gods. The Beatitudes have shown us those misinterpretations; but, as we have seen, the right use of instincts is not to destroy them but to heal and fulfill them.

There is true wealth as well as illusory: "If riches be desired in life, what is richer than wisdom, which maketh all things?"[197]

There is true power as well as false: "If, then, your delight be in thrones and scepters, O ye kings of the people, love wisdom, that you may reign for ever,"[198] "for she is a vapor of the power of God," she "can do all things," and no evil can overcome her.

[196] Wisd. 8:1.
[197] Wisd. 8:5.
[198] Wisd. 6:22.

There is true glory as well as the glory that is vain: "For her sake I shall have glory among the multitude, and honor with the ancients, though I be young."[199]

There is true pleasure, joy, and comfort: "When I go into my house I shall repose myself with her: for her conversation hath no bitterness, nor her company any tediousness, but joy and gladness; and she will be a comfort in my cares and grief";[200] she is "more beautiful than the sun, and above all the order of the stars."

There is that life of action which is not a distraction from the end, but an expression of it: "And if a man love justice, her labors have great virtues"; and "if understanding is effective, who is a more artful worker than she of those things that are?"[201]

There is a desire for knowledge, understanding, and vision: "All such things as are hidden and not foreseen I have learned: for wisdom, which is the worker of all things, taught me."[202]

And lastly there is the hunger for that true peace which the world cannot give: and we read that by wisdom "I shall set the people in order, and nations shall be subject to me";[203] and that, where the inner peace of the spirit is concerned, "by wisdom they were healed, whosoever hath pleased Thee, O Lord, from the beginning," and it is in wisdom that "thou shalt find rest in the latter end."[204]

[199] Wisd. 8:10.

[200] Wisd. 8:16, 9.

[201] Wisd. 8:7, 6.

[202] Wisd. 7:21.

[203] Wisd. 8:14.

[204] Wisd. 9:19; Ecclus. 6:29.

But how are all these things made one, and how are they to be acquired? "This also was a point of wisdom, to know whose gift it was. I went to the Lord, and besought Him, and said with my whole heart: 'God of my fathers and Lord of mercy . . . give me wisdom that sitteth by Thy throne. . . . For I am Thy servant and the son of Thy handmaid, a weak man and of short time, and falling short of the understanding of judgment and laws. For if one be perfect among the children of men, yet if Thy wisdom be not with him, he shall be nothing regarded.' "[205] This is the wisdom which is "from above."

Divine wisdom is the greatest wisdom

Wisdom in general, as we have seen, is not in a vast store of information, nor in scientific knowledge; it is not the same thing as critical ability; and it is not to be acquired simply by character training. It is the knowledge of things by their highest and ultimate causes.

But again there are degrees of wisdom. You can have that wisdom which is natural knowledge of natural things: we call it philosophy, and it is very great, but there is greater wisdom than that. You can have that sort of wisdom which is discursive knowledge of supernatural things: we call it theology, and it is greater but not the greatest. You can have also that divine wisdom which is supernatural experience of supernatural reality: and this is the utmost height of the human spirit on earth because it is not just reason-knowledge, but love-knowledge. It is a direct if obscure union with the Infinite, the knowledge

[205] Wisd. 9:1-6.

of the highest things in the sense that the knower is one in the depths of his being with the Known. *Patiens divina:* he knows because he *experiences* divine things.

That is why from this wisdom there is peace: because in it all desires are made aspects of one desire. There is joy, because in it there is a sense of the solution of even the hardest and deepest problems of evil and pain. There is abundance of life, because this wisdom is itself oneness with the Infinite life. And there is abundance of power, because to experience divine things is to have the cosmic energy of redemption within the self.

Mary is the supreme expression of divine wisdom

"I went to the Lord and besought Him." The wisdom from above is spoken of in the feminine; the word itself is feminine. For this is not the masculine science and power of governance which are conquered or acquired; it is the wisdom that is received from above, given in love, not taken possession of by the soul so much as brought forth in the soul that is possessed by divinity.

The soul is female to God. The Son is the Wisdom of the Father: the Man, but also the Eternal Child. But among creatures it is Mary who is the supreme expression and symbol of divine wisdom, for in woman you have the identification of child-life and maturity.

Mary the Mother, Mary the Bride: the first is the epitome of all human experience, the Mother of Sorrows, the Queen of the Seven Swords; the epitome of all that ordering of things, but ordering sweetly, which is motherhood; and the epitome of all the care, responsibility, and compassion of the bearer for the born. But the second title is the key to the depth, the stillness, and the wonder. It is what turns experience into gentleness, understanding into compassion, governance into sweetness, responsibility into compassion, and sorrow into joy. In the eyes of the mother is the understanding of "the beginning, and ending, and midst of the times";[206] but they are also and forever the eyes of the girl, the bride, who says, "He that is mighty hath done great things in me."[207]

To be like Mary, you must have wisdom and be able to say, "I understand"; but to be able to say that, you must first say with her, "Teach me."

Divine wisdom makes us kind and gentle

The soul is female to God. You must use fully the mental power God has given you; you must acquire wisdom and acquire it not least by the hard road of human experience. But you need, more than all this, the wisdom from above, and that wisdom can only be given to you.

It is the divine wisdom that can "dispose all things sweetly," that knows compassion as well as order. The man who is unsure of himself and his knowledge or competence blusters and bullies. The wise man is gentle with other minds because he understands them; he is patient with their defects because he is sure of his own ground. He has the patience of divine tolerance — which is very different from the unprincipled

[206] Wisd. 7:18.
[207] Luke 1:49.

tolerance which makes no distinction between truth and falsehood — because he always takes the long view, and he knows that good can come eventually from evil and truth from falsehood. He can be compassionate and can help instead of condemning because he understands with what obstacles the human mind and heart have to contend. His is not the remote unreality of the academic philosopher nor the immersion in the world of time of the superficial pleasure-seeker: he is wholly in the eternal present because he lives in wisdom who "remaineth in herself the same," but he is wholly in the world of time also, because his wisdom is the wisdom that serves the world.

To dispose all things *sweetly:* that is the test of the divine wisdom in practice. "Charity is kind,"[208] says St. Paul; and Ruysbroeck tells us simply: "Be kind, be kind, and you will be saints." That is the quality in the wisdom of the saints that gives them their power — the power to compel others to love what they love.

We are destined for union with God

Wisdom is the fruit of love: we judge things as though with the eyes of God because we are *one* with God. "An emanation of the glory": the men of prayer have spoken of the spirit of man as a *scintilla Dei,* a spark thrown off, as it were, from the infinite globe of fire, created into separateness (the spark is not the fire, the finite is not the Infinite) and yet destined, while still retaining its self-identity, to return into the greater life of

[208] 1 Cor. 13:4.

the One and the All, for only there can it find its own fullness, its complete enhancement and glory, of being.

Is this return a thing which only Heaven can fulfill? Perfectly, yes: it can be fulfilled completely only in the glory of the Light inaccessible, when the eyes of the spirit behold face to face the Unimaginable and are rapt in timeless ecstasy.

But there are some who have known Heaven on earth: a beginning of beatitude is possible even this side the grave. The divine life into which the sons of God are reborn confers on them a new power: the power to apprehend the Godhead Itself, present within them, as immediate object of knowledge and love. God is present within them, not only as Creator of all that the soul is, but as that with which the spirit can be truly united and which the spirit can truly and immediately *experience*. "He that cleaveth to the Lord is *one spirit*."[209]

Those who have experienced these divine things tell us, insofar as human language can, how real and close a union this is. It is not yet to be described in terms of vision: that cannot be while they are still living the life of faith; but they convey to us something of its immediacy and intimacy by speaking of it in terms of the sense of touch. There is something much more here than the silence of deep understanding: it is the silence of the love that is too deep for words: "Lost to all things and myself, and amid the lilies forgotten."

You are here in a realm beyond ideas: "What agony," says St. Teresa, "for the soul to return to reason." You are in the realm of the highest form of love-knowledge, apart from the vision of God.

[209] 1 Cor. 6:17.

In the prayer of union, the soul is absorbed in God

Think for a moment of human ecstasy: the word conveys the idea of being "outside the self," because the intensity of love and joy is such as to fill the self completely and exclusively with the realization of the other, and of the greater life into which one is thus caught up and transformed. There is a real, if momentary, self-oblivion, a forgetfulness too of everything except this immediate and wholly absorbing reality, and perhaps for this moment the whole personality is really made one, whole, and wholly expressive in a wordless affirmation of surrender to this greater reality into which it is absorbed. In some such terms the mystics have described the reality of the prayer of union: the absorption, the oblivion of everything except the supreme Reality, the sense of oneness, the sense of utter fullness of spirit — "I have found Him whom my soul loveth: I have held Him, and I will not let Him go."[210]

Sometimes the intensity of this experience produces those physical effects which are too often supposed to be the essentials of the highest states of prayer. They are entirely irrelevant and accidental; they merely mean that the body is not strong enough to bear the experience given, the life imparted. They are on the same level as the momentary loss of consciousness which can be produced by any intense joy or sorrow. The essence of the prayer of union is precisely the *union* of spirit with Spirit.

But we have to remember, also, that this supreme experience must, of its nature, be transitory: there are limits to the

[210] Song of Sol. 3:4.

joy as well as the suffering that human beings can bear. It can be no more than a moment in life, but of course it must necessarily color and transform the rest of life. For the moment, you leave the prayer of petition and sorrow and the rest, but only for the moment. Wisdom is "more active than all active things": if you are given this supreme prayer, it is as a sharing in Christ's eternal adoration of the Father, and therefore as a sharing also in His redemption of the world.

Wisdom enables us to share more fully in Christ's redemptive work

We come back to the Christian ideal of action as the overflow and expression of contemplation: if you are caught up in the power of the Spirit even to the seventh Heaven, it is so that you may then share more fully, with greater power, in the redemptive activity of Christ in the world.

Father Vincent McNabb,[211] preaching to some of his fellow Dominicans, once said: "The world is waiting for those who love it; if you don't love the world, don't preach to it: preach to yourself." The primary thing, if you are to be a preacher, is to have the truth; and since we all in some way preach (although not perhaps in words) it is the truth that we primarily need. But for your preaching to have a deep and lasting effect, you need more than an intellectual apprehension of the truth; you need the wisdom from above, the wisdom that makes you one with the truth in heart as well as in mind. Then you have the power that can hope to drive out prejudice and

[211] Dominican priest and writer (1868-1943).

make way for the truth: you have that inner power which is love, which draws all things to Christ.

"She is more beautiful than the sun and . . . being compared with the light, she is found before it. For after this cometh night; but no evil can overcome wisdom." When you have the wisdom of the Spirit, you have the source itself of all serenity; you have also the fine flower of fortitude. Nothing can overcome it: you are not worried as to what you shall say, for what you shall say is given to you; you are not dismayed by obstacles, for you know that you live in the life and power of Him who has overcome the world, Him with whom all things are possible. So you yourself are still with the stillness of deep night, yet more active than all active things because of the fire that blazes in you, and from you to the world.

"Being but one, she can do all things, and remaining in herself the same, she reneweth all things." So we pray in the prayer to the Holy Spirit: *Send forth Thy Spirit and they shall be re-created, and Thou shalt renew the face of the earth.* And so, when we have asked for the gift of true wisdom, we go on to ask for what necessarily goes with it; that we may always *"rejoice in His holy consolations" — His strengthening solace and renewal — through Christ our Lord. Amen.*

C. The Sacrament of this Beatitude

The Priesthood

For winter is now past, the rain is over and gone. The flowers have appeared in our land: the time of pruning is come: the voice of the turtledove is heard in our land.[212]

It is the old traditional Catholic doctrine that all the faithful share in the priesthood of Christ.[213] Let us think briefly, first of all, of what the official priesthood means. We shall then be able to apply something of what we have discovered to the common priesthood of the laity in which we all must share.

The essence of the priesthood is the power to say Mass: to be the mouthpiece of the words of consecration, which change the bread and wine into the Body and Blood of Christ, and then to administer to the faithful the Sacrament of the sacrificed Christ. And why? It is because essentially the Church is the torrent of divine life and power which flows ceaselessly into the world, to heal and restore it. As all the other functions of the priesthood (the teaching office, the pastoral charge, and the administration of the other sacraments) are grouped about

[212] Song of Sol. 2:11-12.
[213] Cf. 1 Pet. 2:5.

and center in this supreme office of offering Mass, so all of the things which make up the Church's life (doctrinal, pastoral, and disciplinary) are aspects of this essential fact, that the Church is the continuation of the Christ-life on earth — teaching, healing, and empowering. It is the storehouse of the energy and power of good which must combat the power of evil to the end, and which, as it triumphs over the dark power, makes all things new.

But that means that the apostolate is of the essence of the Church's life, because it is bound up with the Eucharist. The duty of the priest is first to say, "*Hoc est Corpus meum,*" "This is my Body," turning to God with the people; but then he must say also, "*Hoc est Corpus Eius,*" "This is His Body," turning to the people with God. And as we have seen, it is the whole of creation that must be brought to the Mass to be healed and sanctified: beyond the immediate assistants there is the whole body of the faithful; beyond the faithful there is the whole of creation, still in travail even until now. So, in order to express the priesthood and the Church in general, you have to think of a double duty: to bring God to the world, to bring the world to God.

The common priesthood is one of service

In that double movement the laity share. The old doctrine of the common priesthood has found in these latter days a new expression in terms of Catholic Action. The priest is, in an official sense, a mediator, turning to God with the people, turning to the people with God. But the whole company of the faithful must also mediate in a different way, turning first to

God as a family, a unity, and then, still a family, turning in the life and power of God to the greater family of mankind and all creation, witnessing, blessing, showing forth the abundance of life, power, and love and, through them, drawing all things to Christ.

But again this mediatorship is centered in the Mass: it is a sacrificial life that is to be shown, not self-consciously but powerfully, to the world. That is the essence of the common priesthood. "We are all anointed into one holy priesthood," says St. Ambrose,[214] "whenever we offer ourselves as sacrifices to God." And St. Leo[215] asks: "What is there so priestly . . . as to bring to God from the altar of the heart the immaculate sacrifice of Christian piety?" The common priesthood is the priesthood of service: a service sanctified by the spirit of worship and of sacrifice.

Inner prayer must drive social action

Once again we return to the Christian view of the life of action as the overflow and expression of contemplation. If the phrase "Catholic Action" is interpreted as meaning that the way to serve the Church is to be endlessly active and to let contemplation take care of itself, then the glory of the common priesthood will necessarily be lost. There must always be enough inner life to vivify the external life of action; otherwise it will be weak, superficial, and perhaps harmful, however much goodwill may be put into it.

[214] Bishop of Milan and Doctor of the Church (c. 339-397).

[215] St. Leo the Great (d. 461), Pope and Doctor of the Church.

You share in the priesthood of Christ first of all if you share in the prayer of Christ. There are some in the Church whose whole function is to be, in a phrase of Père Sertillanges,[216] "beings of praise": the contemplative religious whose primary work is the *opus Dei* ("the work of God"), the Liturgy. They are, in a special sense, the Church's worship, and therefore the Church's powerhouse; but their life is something in which we all have to share. Whenever you assist at Mass or at the Divine Office, whenever you pray within the framework of the total prayer of the Church, as you always in fact, as a Christian, do, you join in that official act of worship, and you share in the primary function of being the storehouse of the divine power.

But to do that is itself an apostolate, and the necessary condition of all other apostolic activities. Worship is an apostolate because it is a worship of love: we cannot pray as Christians at all unless in our prayer the travail of all creation is at least implicitly expressed. But then, when this primary condition of prayer is at least beginning to be fulfilled, it is possible to turn to the priesthood of service: bringing God to the world, not in the official and literal manner of the priest with the Eucharist, but in the sense that the service of love spreads light and joy in the world, and the light is the Life.

We share in the common priesthood in our work

To feed the hungry and give drink to the thirsty, to clothe the naked and shelter the homeless: all these works of mercy

[216] Antonin Gilbert Sertillanges (1863-1948), French Dominican priest, scholar, and writer.

are ways of sharing in the common priesthood, and so are all the ways in which the faithful take their immensely important share in the work of making known the truth of the gospel and the love that the gospel reveals.

The tasks of the common priesthood change with the changing circumstances of life: perhaps the type of all such tasks today is the sacrificial work which attempts to redeem industrialism from within, in the power of Christ the Worker. But all work can be in some degree a fulfillment of this priesthood, provided always that it is turned into worship and so becomes the expression of love.

And again the two things, work and worship, are mutually interactive: you make your worship complete when you make it a part of your work for the world; you make your work complete when you turn it into loving service of the world and so into worship of the Redeemer of the world. You can praise Him with harp and timbrel. But you can praise Him, too, as Mary His mother did, with all the common daily work of your hands, with all the cares and drudgery, and with all the fun and laughter that come your way, if you take these things as a love-gift from Him and make them a love-gift to your family.

The love of those in the religious life embraces the whole world

But the Christian's family, once again, is the world. There can be no limit to the scope of apostolic activity, because of the divine immensity of charity.

There is a difference here between those who are called to the sacrament of marriage and those who are called to the religious life of the cloister. These latter must, *ex officio*, substitute for a life of love rounded immediately by their own particular home (even though, as we have seen, the home has its vocation in the world beyond) a life of love which immediately embraces all humanity. There is no need to stress their tremendous need of abundance of life and power. Perhaps it is easy to love all humanity in the abstract — and from the point of view of humanity it is likely to be valueless; but to love all humanity in the concrete, to love all men and women, is beyond the power of man. How, then, are they to hope for the life and the power? Because of the special relationship in which, if they are faithful to their calling, they stand to God.

In the normal way, men and women are completed in marriage. But notice that this substantial completion is of its nature limited: you are completed in this particular framework of love and shared life, and it is your boundary, even though it then looks beyond itself.

The religious life has no such limitation, glorious though that limitation is: the monk and the nun miss the normal way of completion, and if they misunderstand their vocation, they become in consequence shrunken and desiccated; but if they understand it aright and are faithful to the last ounce of their energy, they find not a loss but an immeasurable gain. St. Thomas is accustomed to speak of God as possessing the qualities or powers of creatures *virtualiter eminenter*: not having the thing itself as it is in us, since that would be a limitation, but having it virtually, having the power of producing the same effect, and having it in a pre-eminent way, since what, for example, is for us a matter of energy and labor is for Him simply the effortless *fiat* of infinite will. So it is with those who are called to forgo the completion of married life: their denial is but an aspect of a far greater affirmation; for the fullness of life which married love brings to these others is meant to be found for them in the greater fullness of their life with God.

And it is a fullness which of its nature is such as to be expressed not in the small world of the home, but in the universality of creation. They, too, are meant to share a life of love, and be completed by it; but it is a love whose purpose and fulfillment alike are not *these* children begotten of *this* father, but *all* created things, the children of the heavenly Father. So they can give all to the world because they have been given all by God. Their vocation is to be identified with Mary in her universal compassion because they are to be identified with her in her divine wisdom. And they are to share this divine wisdom because they are to share with her the prayer of union: they are to share with her, although in so different a way, that immediacy of relationship between themselves and the Spirit which implies a complete possession by the Spirit — a possession which completes them precisely as accepting, and feeling responsibility for, all created things as their own.

The common priesthood calls us all to a life of union with God and the world

All that is the special glory, and the terrifying responsibility, of the priest and the religious. But we all must share in it, because we all must share in the common priesthood of the faithful.

Married love has its own immediate and essential purpose; but, as we have seen, it looks beyond itself to the world without, and it looks to the world without because it first looks up to God. We are all called to the substance of the prayer of union and the life of union; and human love is only fulfilled when it is part of that mightier love, when the single living spark that is two-in-unity returns to the infinite Fire. And then, so enhanced, empowered, and intensified, it returns to the world of men, to share in its own particular way in the universal love and universal compassion. This love and compassion, it is true, are to be shown for the most part implicitly, or at least within the relatively small circle of immediate neighbors and friends, but nonetheless, they cannot be circumscribed, cannot be limited to any circle, nation, or race, in the inner readiness of the heart to love and serve.

That is why in married life there must be the spirit of the three monastic vows: there must be poverty of spirit; there must be the chastity of the temperate and the clean of heart; and there must be the obedience of those who love all the things that God loves, and whose joy is to fulfill His will in serving them.

Mary is the model of the Beatitudes

The soul is female to God. Our Lady is the universal Mother in this sense also: that we all have to learn from her, as from a model, of what we are to be. The whole train of thought we have been following through these pages is fulfilled pre-eminently in her.

Think of the glorious song of praise that she sang when Elizabeth saluted the majesty of her motherhood: it is a triumphant assertion of the rebirth of mankind into the new and infinite life. The winter is past, the rain is over and gone, because man is no longer doomed to the misery of loneliness; the Center of life is restored to him; he can be fulfilled to infinity because he can lose his life, to find it again in God. If you read through the verses of the *Magnificat*,[217] you find in them almost a summary of the Beatitudes; you find certainly that ringing note of love, wonder, humility, and happiness about which they tell us.

"My soul doth magnify the Lord, and my spirit hath rejoiced in God my Savior": at the very beginning there is the primary lesson of poverty of spirit, the fixing of the eyes not on the self but on God.

"Because He hath regarded the humility of His handmaid" (the meekness of the truly happy), "for behold from henceforth all generations shall call me blessed." How she must have trembled as she spoke the lovely boast, trembled with love and wonder, but most of all with the bewilderment of humility: for it is "because He that is mighty hath done great things in me; and holy is His name.

"And His mercy" — His comfort — "is from generation to generation, to them that fear Him" — and fearing, are able to mourn.

"He hath shewed might in His arm: He hath scattered the proud in the conceit of their heart. He hath put down the mighty" — those who seek not the inner power of love but the external might that feeds pride and is fed by injustice — "from their seat and hath exalted the humble," the little ones, the clean of heart who have the docility of the child.

[217] Luke 1:46-55.

"He hath filled the hungry with good things" — those who are hungry because of their suffering of injustice, those who mourn, those who hunger and thirst after justice — "and the rich," those who treat created things as means to their own pleasure or profit, "He hath sent empty away. He hath received Israel His servant, being mindful of His mercy" because to be a servant, to be a humble instrument of His mercy, and so to bring to the world His life, light, and peace, is in itself to receive His mercy in all its fullness. You must struggle and fight and persevere with all your strength; but when you think that any success, any goodness, is achieved you must say, "*He* that is mighty hath done great things *in me*, and holy is *His* name."

"For I am Thy servant and the son of Thy handmaid, a weak man, and of short time, and falling short of the understanding of judgment and laws." Mary is the universal Mother, and therefore we her children are to try to model ourselves upon her; "for it is she," as is said of the wisdom with which the Church identifies her, "that teacheth the knowledge of God";[218] it is she who in her gesture of humble and proud acceptance at the Annunciation symbolizes for us the response of the creature to the healing and ennobling touch of God. From her we learn to be happy, for in her is the selfless poverty of spirit that makes her a mother, the childlike meekness that makes her the Virgin Bride of the Infinite, the sacrificial mourning that gives her the strength of the Tower of Ivory and makes her the Cause of our Joy, the hunger and thirst for God's will that makes her the Mirror of Justice, the compassion that makes her the Comfort of the Afflicted, the cleanness of heart

[218] Wisd. 8:4.

that makes her the Seat of Wisdom, and the flawless inner peace that entitles her to be called the Queen of Peace.

And those who know that to love and revere her is only to do greater honor to her Son, also greet her with one of the loveliest of her titles, the Morning Star, the star that heralds the dawn of the Word in the world. For it is through the birth of her Son that the whole world is reborn and renewed; it is through the glory of her selfless *magnificat* that the Light comes into the world and makes all things new.

In her, therefore, is all the joy of the life of worship: because what was lost is recovered, what was dead is quickened to new life; because even in spite of sin and suffering, the world is lovely again, for His feet have trodden it; because winter is now past, the rain is over and gone, and the flowers have appeared in our land — and in the priestly bestowal of life which brings about the reflowering of the earth, she and all her children who follow her share and are glorified. Finally, in her is all the joy of worship because this is not an end but a beginning, the joyful sacrifice that precedes the eternal banquet and must be offered until the end, when the day breaks and the shadows retire.

For beyond there lies the fullness of glory, the blazing splendor of the Sun of the eternal noon, the new Heaven and new earth that are the tabernacle of God with men. And He shall wipe away all tears from their eyes, and there shall be neither mourning nor crying nor any other sorrow, for the former things shall have passed away, and they shall see His face, and night shall be no more.[219]

[219] Rev. 21:3-4.

Biographical note

Biographical note

Gerald Vann

(1906-1963)

Born in England in 1906, Gerald Vann entered the Dominican Order in 1923 and, after completing his theological studies in Rome, was ordained a priest in 1929. On returning to England, he studied modern philosophy at Oxford and was then sent to Blackfriars School in Northhamptonshire to teach and later to serve as headmaster of the school and as superior of the community there. Tireless in his efforts to bolster the foundations of peace, he organized the international Union of Prayer for Peace during his tenure at Blackfriars.

Fr. Vann devoted his later years to writing, lecturing, and giving retreats in England and in the United States, including lecturing at Catholic University of America in Washington, DC. He wrote numerous articles and books, including a biography of St. Thomas Aquinas, who influenced him greatly.

Fr. Vann's writings combine the philosophy and theology of St. Thomas with the humanism emphasized in the 1920s and 1930s. His works reflect his keen understanding of man's relationship to God, his deep sensitivity to human values, and his compassionate understanding of man's problems and needs. Particularly relevant in today's divided world is his appeal for unity, charity, and brotherhood. His words reveal what it means today to fulfill the two greatest commandments: to love God and to love one's neighbor.

Sophia Institute Press®

Sophia Institute Press®

Sophia Institute is a nonprofit institution that seeks to restore man's knowledge of eternal truth, including man's knowledge of his own nature, his relation to other persons, and his relation to God.

Sophia Institute Press® serves this end in numerous ways. It publishes translations of foreign works to make them accessible for the first time to English-speaking readers. It brings back into print books that have been long out of print. And it publishes important new books that fulfill the ideals of Sophia Institute. These books afford readers a rich source of the enduring wisdom of mankind.

Sophia Institute Press® makes these high-quality books available to the general public by using advanced technology and by soliciting donations to subsidize its general publishing costs.

Your generosity can help Sophia Institute Press® provide the public with editions of works containing the enduring wisdom of the ages. Please send your tax-deductible contribution to the address on the following page.

The members of the Editorial Board of Sophia Institute Press® welcome questions, comments, and suggestions from all our readers.

For your free catalog, call:

Toll-free: 1-800-888-9344

or write:

Sophia Institute Press®

Box 5284

Manchester, NH 03108

Internet users may visit our website at

http://www.sophiainstitute.com

Sophia Institute is a tax-exempt institution as defined by the Internal Revenue Code, Section 501(c)(3).

Tax I.D. 22-2548708.